SECURE YOUR RETIREMENT DREAMS

$AFE MONEY
WITH

**Build a Retirement Plan That Will Stand the Test of Time
Without Losing Your Money on the Wall Street Roller Coaster**

SECURE YOUR RETIREMENT DREAMS
WITH
$AFE MONEY

**Build a Retirement Plan That Will Stand the Test of Time
Without Losing Your Money on the Wall Street Roller Coaster**

BY

BRENT TYCKSEN

WITH

TERRY KEYZER

SECURE YOUR RETIREMENT DREAMS WITH SAFE MONEY:
Build a Retirement Plan That Will Stand the Test of Time Without
Losing Your Money on the Wall Street Roller Coaster

ISBN: 978-1519240897

Printed in the United States of America
Year of First Printing: 2015

Disclaimer: The Publisher and the Authors make no representations or warranties with
respect to the accuracy or completeness of the contents of this work and specifically disclaim
all warranties, including without limitation warranties of fitness for a particular purpose.
No warranty may be created or extended by sales or promotional materials. The advice and
strategies contained herein may not be suitable for every situation. This work is sold with
the understanding that the Publisher is not engaged in rendering legal, accounting, or other
professional services. If professional assistance is required, the services of a competent
professional person should be sought. Neither the Publisher nor the Authors shall be liable
for damages arising therefrom.
  The fact that an organization or website is referred to in this work as a citation and/or
a potential source of further information does not mean that the Authors or the Publisher
endorses the information the organization or website may provide or recommendations it
may make. Further, readers should be aware that Internet websites listed in this work may
have changed or disappeared between when this work was written and when it is read.
While great efforts have been taken to provide accurate and current information regarding
the covered material, neither Brent Tycksen nor Safe Money Associates are responsible for
any errors or omissions, or for the results obtained from the use of this information.

From Terry:

I would like to dedicate this to God, Bobby, and my family.

From Brent:

To Mom and Dad, for teaching me the value of hard work and the necessity of play.

To my brothers and sister, for your friendship as youth that continues now as we all experience being grandparents, and for being great examples in our entrepreneurial endeavors.

To our four exceptional children, who put up with Dad working long hours.

To our wonderful grandchildren, who love "Papa" and "Grum" unconditionally.

I especially want to thank my wife, who is as beautiful inside as she is outside, and who has put up with me for the forty-two years we have known each other and our thirty-seven years of marriage. You are the love of my life and my eternal companion. You make me want to be a better man. Van ewigheid tot ewigheid.

CONTENTS

For the Doubting Thomas   1

Section 1: Killing the Status Quo   5

Chapter 1: Cancer, Cures, and Killing the Status Quo   7
Chapter 2: Saying Goodbye to the Stock Market   19

Section 2: A New World   29

Chapter 3: Instant Gratification and Taking Advice from Gurus   31
Chapter 4: Willie Sutton and the Tax Man   37
Chapter 5: Killing the Interest Vampire   47

Section 3: Creating a Safe Money Foundation   55

Chapter 6: Defeating the Enemies of Wealth   57
Chapter 7: Finance Your Own Prosperity™   69
Chapter 8: Super Charging the 7702 Plan™   91

Section 4: Does It Work?   101

Chapter 9: Disney, J.C. Penney, McDonald's, and You:
            Making It Work   103
Chapter 10: God's Miracle: I've Been Restored!   121
Chapter 11: Bonus: For Business Owners Only   125

            Free Bonus Content   131
            Acknowledgement   133
            7702 Plan ™ Analysis Request Form   135
            Endnotes   137
            About the Authors   139

For the Doubting Thomas

I don't blame you. There are thousands of books out there that claim, "This is the way!" Before you read my book, let me share with you a few questions that I have been asked:

Is it really possible to build a Safe Money Retirement Plan?

Actually, it depends. It's not for everyone. Some people are addicted to the ups and downs of the market—and believe it or not, they can't understand how their money can safely grow each and every day regardless of the economy, market, or latest bad news on TV. If that's you, sorry—now is the time to shut the cover of this book and pass it on to someone who wants some security and peace of mind in their financial future.

Is it too late for me?

No way! No matter what your age, the concepts embraced by Safe Money professionals can be used to grow and safeguard your money for you or your family at any point in time.

Do I have to scrimp and save and basically eat beans and rice in order to grow my money?

Nope. No dietary changes are required to join the club. In fact, once you discover how to Finance Your Own Prosperity, you may just end up living better while saving money doing it. There's nothing like living the high life without the heavy dose of guilt or pressure of too-tight budget.

Is this just more pop culture investment advice?

This book is for anyone who is sick of the stomach turning ups and downs of what I like to call the "Wall Street Roller Coaster". The principles taught in this book have been around for years. Case studies range from startup business owners to the average American household and anywhere in between. If you're sick of the status quo and are ready to stop drinking the financial guru Kool-Aid, this book is for you.

Is this just another financial dead end? How do I know whom to trust?

Fortunately for all of us, the solutions I share with you in this book have been around for over a hundred years. In fact, there's a good chance your parents or even your grandparents used some of these lost strategies decades ago…you might say we're bringing some financial wisdom back from the dead!

Do I need to be a financial whiz?

Not at all. In fact, I think you'll find the whole process refreshingly simple – no monitoring the markets and no complex calculations to worry about. Once you get going, building a Safe Money Retirement Plan can happen almost on autopilot.

So what is a Safe Money Retirement Plan? Here's what it isn't: stuffing your money in your mattress or hunkering down with gold bullion. You don't even need to have a million bucks to be in the club. Building a Safe Money Retirement Plan means you've started on a low-risk path that will keep your money safely growing over time – guaranteed. Rest assured, for the average America, the dream of becoming a millionaire is not out of reach. In Fact, the blueprint is sitting in your hands right now. So turn the page and start reading.

SECTION 1

KILLING THE STATUS QUO

"Status quo, you know—that is Latin for 'the mess we're in.'"
— Ronald Reagan

"Bureaucracy defends the status quo long past the time when the quo has lost its status."
—Dr. Laurence J. Peter

CHAPTER 1

CANCER, CURES, AND KILLING THE STATUS QUO

I am the second-oldest son of six boys and one girl. I was raised by hard-working parents who believed in teaching their children a good, strong work ethic. We had animals, chickens, a vegetable garden, fruit trees, a raspberry patch, and grape vines. We had to care for the animals, milk the goats, gather the eggs, weed and care for our assigned rows in the garden—along with numerous other chores—each and every day. We had to do this before we could go play with our friends. All summer long, we would water, weed, and care for the garden. In the fall, we would pick corn, dig potatoes, dig carrots, and pick apples, peaches, and pears. Then we would help our parents prepare and preserve the harvest by bottling the perishables and putting the potatoes, carrots, apples, and squash into the root cellar properly so they wouldn't spoil.

We were very self-sufficient. We had to be. Although my dad had a good job, we were a large family and didn't have a lot of discretionary income. The literal fruits of our labors would feed us during the winter so we would have funds for new school clothes, shoes, and other necessities.

My parents told us Aesop's Fables and other similar stories on a regular basis. One that I heard a lot was "The Ant and the Grasshopper." It goes like this:

In a field one summer's day, a grasshopper was hopping about, chirping and singing to its heart's content. An ant passed by, bearing along with great toil an ear of corn he was taking to the nest.

"Why not come and chat with me," said the grasshopper, "instead of toiling and moiling in that way?"

"I am helping to lay up food for the winter," said the ant, "and recommend you to do the same."

"Why bother about winter?" said the grasshopper. "We have plenty of food at present." But the ant went on its way and continued its toil.

When the winter came, the grasshopper had no food and found itself dying of hunger, while it saw the ants distributing corn and grain from the stores they had collected in the summer. Then the grasshopper knew: It is best to prepare for the days of necessity.

I remember one time when it was my responsibility to prepare the fresh straw in the bottom of the root cellar so the potatoes, carrots, and apples would not spoil during the long winter. One of my friends came by and encouraged me to hurry so I could go play football with the guys. Instead of replacing all the straw, I just spread a little fresh straw over the top of the old, moist, mildewed straw. From the top, it looked like I had done the job right. But underneath, the mold and mildew had already established a foothold and were infiltrating the new straw. I definitely cut corners so I could go play football with my friends. I don't remember who won the game, but I do remember having to haul out all the rotten potatoes, carrots, and apples in the middle of the winter instead of enjoying them in soups, stews, and pies. My dad took the opportunity to remind me again of the ant and the grasshopper. Unfortunately, as a youth, I was the grasshopper more than I should have been.

As a nineteen-year-old, I had the opportunity to volunteer for two years in southern Africa. Wow, what an eye-opening experience for a young man to live in some of the most technologically advanced countries, and also some of the poorest third-world countries on the planet. In Mozambique and Malawi, starvation and poverty were rampant. Robert Mugabe and his guerilla fighters were terrorizing everyone in Rhodesia (now Zimbabwe). They wanted to take over the government and socialize everything. There would be no rich and no poor. Everyone would have the same amount.

After my two years of service, I returned home, went to school, got married, started a family, and also started several businesses. The teachings of my parents' home were indelibly imprinted on my life. I could be anything I wanted to be, if I was willing to work for it. No one was going to take care of me and my family but me and my family. It's best to prepare for the days of necessity. Oh, yeah . . . work hard and play hard, each at the right time.

My wife and I have been blessed with four wonderful children, and to date, five beautiful grandchildren. We have passed on to them the lessons we learned from our parents and grandparents. In our thirty-seven years of marriage, we have started several successful businesses, and a few that were not as successful. We have always tried to prepare for the days of necessity.

Our first Christmas together, we were poor college students. We gave each other a set of cookware and some food for our pantry. I remember the extravagance of a case of cream of mushroom soup, twenty-four cans of tuna fish, and a ten-pound bag of curly noodles—all part of a family-favorite tuna casserole recipe. Our Christmas present to ourselves helped sustain us as we finished school.

In 2004, I found a lump in my neck. After several diagnostic procedures, we were told that I had stage four thyroid cancer. My thyroid was one giant tumor. The cancer had also spread into my lymph system. I remember the doctor telling us, "I'm not looking for cancer anymore—I'm looking to see how far it has spread." Several weeks later, skilled surgeons removed my thyroid and as many cancerous lymph nodes as they could. After two months of recovery, they started a prolonged radiation treatment regime. Thyroid cancer is slow-growing, so they spread the treatment out over several years. They gave me a high "killer" dose of radiation to destroy as many cancer cells as they could, then let me recover. They used a nuclear medicine scanning device, similar to an MRI, to track where the radiation was being absorbed, to see how far the cancer had spread, and to determine how much had been killed. That was not a fun experience.

The doctor told us that after I ingested the radiation, I needed to stay at least ten feet away from any living thing for two weeks. Those ten feet included through walls, floors, and ceilings. I was banished to a guest room on the top floor of our home, as far away from everyone as possible. We wrapped everything in the room in plastic to protect it so any radioactive body oils, etc. could be disposed of without permanently destroying the item.

Thyroid cells are the only things in our body that will absorb iodine, so oncologists use radioactive iodine to treat thyroid cancer. In order to prepare your body to absorb the iodine, they starve your body of iodine by removing it from your diet and taking you off any thyroid supplements. Thyroid cancer survivors refer to it as "hypo-hell". The thyroid sends out a hormone called T3 that controls how quickly the body uses energy and makes proteins, among other things. Without the T3, you feel like you have a really bad case of influenza. Your body aches, you have no energy, and you are extremely lethargic.

Once the thyroid cells in your body are craving iodine, the doctors give you the radiation treatment. After the treatment, it takes about five months before the flu-like symptoms are completely gone and your energy level somewhat returns. You have about four months of some normalcy, and then they take you off your synthroid (T3) and prepare your body for another dose of radiation . . . and the cycle starts again. After five years of treatments and diagnostic radiation doses and three years in remission, I am an eight-year survivor and officially cancer free.

I'm explaining this in so much detail because in over thirty years as a financial professional, I have seen many people go through this same scenario in their financial lives. They "invest" their funds in something—usually stocks or mutual funds—it functions in some normalcy for the equivalent of four or five months, and then it adjusts or corrects, they lose money, and they have the equivalent of seven or eight months to recover their money. Then they do it all over again. Sometimes the recovery takes four or five years, not months, to get back to where they were. They are in financial "hypo-hell". Their financial health and well-being are devastated by a form of financial cancer. That cancer is investment risk and investment loss. It's eating away at their assets and future stability. The status quo says you have to put your money at risk in order to get gains. And even though people don't like losing their money, they keep doing it over and over again.

An even bigger form of financial cancer is taxes. The government continues to take more and more to provide for larger entitlement programs and "spreading the wealth." Remember Robert Mugabe? He and his guerrillas finally triumphed in Rhodesia and came into power. In Zimbabwe, interestingly enough, everyone does have the same thing now . . . nothing. Once Mugabe got control of the government, he ruled with an iron fist. He raised taxes on the rich to give to the poor. So the rich left. To stop the outflow, he nationalized everything. The large industrialists and farmers left anyway. Food production diminished exponentially. Things that used to be in abundance are now available in limited supply, usually only on the black market because of inflation and devalued currency.

Just like my thyroid cancer, the financial cancers of investment risk, investment loss, and taxes can be defeated. We do not have to let them destroy our planning for our future and retirement. If Aesop were to write an updated version of the ant and the grasshopper, I believe he would also add the caveat to put the fruit of our preparation somewhere that would be safe and protected from loss to assure that it is there for our use in time of want.

How to Kill the Status Quo

Does any of this "status quo" conventional wisdom sound familiar?

1. Diversify with mutual funds.

2. Max out 401(k) contributions.

3. Keep your credit score high, and shop for low interest rates.

4. Buy term and invest the difference.

5. Put your money in the market to get a good rate of return.

6. Defer taxes until later. (The reality that exposes this myth is really going to blow your mind.)

All this sounds good, but how many folks are really getting ahead financially following this advice? The problem is we're often taking advice from people who may actually be keeping the truth from us for their own profit.

We've heard the same old tired commentary from experts, gurus, and TV personalities for years. Their job isn't to make you wealthy. It's to fill air time and sell advertising. In short, they are paid to crank out microwave money content as fast as they can to keep their magazines or air time full.

Likewise, the conventional wisdom preached from the ivory towers of Wall Street was likely never intended to make the average American wealthy. It's engineered for Wall Street's profit.

So, how well has it worked for the average American?

You probably already know the answer because you live it every day. But let's take a look at the proof:

- Half of all households headed by workers aged fifty-five to sixty-four have less than $88,000 in retirement accounts. [1]

- The average American household with at least one credit card has nearly $10,700 in credit card debt. [2]

- Trillions of dollars have evaporated from 401(k) accounts. [3]

- Of those between 45 and 64, 71 percent admit they are worried about having enough money for retirement. [4]

- The average American is paying up to 34.5 percent of their after-tax income straight to interest. [5]

- In 2010, every three months, 250,000 new homes went into foreclosure. [6]

In addition to grappling with increasing expenses and debt, the average American has been devastated by losses in investments. Today, American Associate of Retired

Persons (AARP) estimates 55 million baby boomers are so concerned about the state of their savings that they are keeping tabs on every penny.

The Jaw-dropping Truth about Wall Street

Who *is* getting rich? The Wall Street firms and their executives, that's who. According to the AFL-CIO in 2009, James Dimon of JP Morgan Chase received $9.2 million in compensation, Goldman Sachs's Lloyd Blankfein received $9.8 in compensation, Wells Fargo's John Stumpf received a jaw-dropping $21.3 million, and Bank of America's Thomas Montag received a mind-blowing $29.9 million for one year's worth of compensation. [7]

Now here's the kicker. These are all banks that received money from the government bailout. The list could go on and on. Go back a few more years to 2005. That year, T. Boone Pickens made $1.4 billion. 1.4 *billion* in compensation in *one* year? [8]

Knocks the wind out of you, doesn't it?

Now don't get me wrong—we don't begrudge someone making a fortune for himself. That's what the American Dream is all about. But where does all that money come from to pay those outrageous CEO paychecks?

Is it from manufacturing a product that is sold to a consumer? Is it from building a home, saving a life in a hospital, or selling groceries at the store?

Nope.

It's from Wall Street working the system with their super computers to profit regardless of whether the market goes up or down. The computers and brokerage houses use lightning-fast algorithms to buy and sell millions of shares a day, executing deals within split seconds. These deals can amount to more than 50 percent of trading volume every day.

Is any real value created by these trades, or is it just a great way to make a lot of money at someone else's expense? These folks create fortunes for themselves, while you, the average citizen, could end up riding the roller coaster of market swings with no control over your money.

But lousy investment returns are just the tip of the iceberg. Another problem is how our money flows—in the front door and out the back without stopping to visit. The average American pays up to 34 percent of his after-tax income in interest charges, saving just a small sliver for himself. [9] If you are like most people who refinance their mortgage a couple times throughout their lives, you likely aren't paying that low, advertised interest rate. You could end up paying as much as 80 percent interest on that mortgage! It's a tried-and-true system set up by bankers to ensure you'll keep paying them interest. (This will be explained in Chapter 5, *Killing the Interest Vampire*.)

One infamous quote was recorded when someone saw a massive yacht club full of million-dollar yachts held exclusively for Wall Street executives. "Where are all the c-c-customer's yachts?" he stammered. [10] Good question.

Seems crazy, doesn't it?

It *is* crazy, but that's the status quo.

But that's not you anymore. You're about to discover a whole new world of money because *you* are ready to join the ranks of those able to retire with Safe Money.

There *is* a way to keep a lot more of your money. There *is* a way you can grow wealthy from your hard work—and keep your money safe at the same time. It's easier than you think. The next few chapters are going to show you how not only to kill the status quo, but also how to join the ranks of those able to retire early with Safe Money. To get started, just turn the page!

CHAPTER 2

SAYING GOODBYE TO THE STOCK MARKET

"If I had to give advice, it would be keep out of Wall Street."
— John D. Rockefeller

Tom Kline wasn't your average teenager.

While most guys were spending their money on video games, Tom was looking at ways to invest. He was fascinated by the idea that invested money could grow automatically, without him having to do anything with it. He bought his first mutual fund when he was fourteen. Yeah, he was pretty different.

He says it all started when he overheard his friend's parents talking about their investment portfolio. He interrupted their conversation and surprised them by asking questions about the market. They explained that anyone could do stocks and that some had even become millionaires. Needless to say, this lit a fire under Tom. Who wouldn't want to make a million dollars?

He'd been saving up his money for a while (told you he was odd) and he had $1500 from mowing lawns and doing odd jobs. He talked to his dad about what he'd learned, and his dad agreed to match his $1500 so he could invest. They chose the stock together and watched it grow over the next five years. When they sold it, it was at a decent profit, which made them both happy—and it had been a fun project for them to do together.

Tom had been bit by the bug.

Over the next few years, he tried several different stocks and strategies, looking to hit on the magic formula. When he heard Warren Buffet share his philosophy, it made sense to him. Essentially, Warren concentrated on consumer monopolies, or what he called "toll bridges". He did his due diligence and then bought the stocks that stood up to his close scrutiny. He bought stocks that were undervalued and held on to them indefinitely, unless something within the structure of the company changed.

Because this made sense to Tom, he started buying stock in large companies like Coca Cola, McDonald's, and Colgate. It makes sense, right? Everyone's got to eat, drink, and brush their teeth.

For five years, Tom did extremely well.

But I bet you can guess what happened then.

The stock market tanked.

And when the market tanks, it takes everything with it.

It doesn't matter that McDonald's and Coke are probably the two most-recognized brands in the world—Tom lost a huge percent of his portfolio. All that money, all that time and research and planning—gone.

Has that ever happened to you, feeling the rug get pulled right out from under your feet and watching it get tossed right over the fence into Niagara Falls?

Say Adios, Wall Street

If you've ever watched a romantic comedy (or paid attention to real life, for that matter), you'll know that any relationship based on deception will end up going down in flames. It doesn't matter how "in love" you are—once that trust is broken, it can take forever (and a whole lot of apologizing) to rebuild.

Tom hadn't lost his heart in an ill-fated romance, but he'd lost about half his shirt on the market. He wasn't about to fall for that line again. He had his moments of nostalgia, remembering how good he had it, but that wasn't enough to convince him to give it yet another go. He knew the market was risky—he wasn't a fool. But seeing it happen so up close and personal was difficult, and he didn't want to experience that again. He wanted something a little more secure, something he could direct and manage. He just didn't know if such a thing existed or if he'd made it all up.

Losing All Your Money Over the Waterfall

Back in May 2010, the Dow Jones Industrial Average was hovering pretty much where it had been 10 years before. Trillions of dollars were lost in stocks, mutual funds, 401(k)s and other qualified plans. The market can

Notable Wall Street Crashes and Recoveries

1901-03
- Fall in the Dow: 46%
- Losses recovered by July 1905
- 2 years to recover

1906-07
- Fall in the Dow: 49%
- Losses recovered by September 1916
- 9 years to recover

1916-17
- Fall in the Dow: 40%
- Losses recovered by November 1919
- 2 years to recover

1919-21
- Fall in the Dow: 47%
- Losses recovered by November 1924
- 3 years to recover

1929-32
- Fall in the Dow: 89%
- Losses recovered by November 1954
- 22 years to recover

1939-42
- Fall in the Dow: 40%
- Losses recovered by January 1945
- 3 years to recover

1973-74
- Fall in the Dow: 45%
- Losses recovered by December 1982
- 8 years to recover

2008-09
- Fall in the Dow: 48%
- Losses recovered by January 2013
- 5 years to recover

be very lucrative during certain periods, but it can turn on you and attack during others. Thousands can be lost in seconds. Do you really want to watch your money get tossed over the waterfall? Can you keep amassing new wealth only to see it get stolen time after time?

Gambling on Wall Street

Every time Tom went to Vegas, he looked around and wondered how the casino owners could afford to build such elaborate establishments. Of course the answer is obvious—the house always wins more than the players. But even though the answer is obvious and everyone knows how easily they could lose, they still go back time after time to try their luck, praying that this time will be "the" time.

And it's the same thing with the market. How many people keep going back to reinvest when they know what a huge risk they're taking?

Would you put all your retirement money on black and pray the roulette wheel would be kind to you? Of course not. That's far too risky, and we can all agree on that. But isn't that remarkably like taking your money down to Wall Street and choosing a stock that will bring it home for you? Horse racing is yet another form of gambling, and choosing the right stock is an awful lot like choosing the right horse.

Don't be like the foolish man who built his house on sand and lost everything—as you make decisions for your financial future, keep one cardinal rule in mind—protect the principal at all costs. Never lose more than you've put in, ever.

Take, for example, a $100,000 investment. Assume the market drops by 30% and your money goes from $100,000 to $70,000. How much growth do you need just to get back to where you started? You might say, "30%," but you'd be wrong. You'd actually need 42.5% growth on your money to get back to where you started. Now how long does it take to see a 30% loss in the market? It could happen in as little as one year. That's not

---

According to the DALBAR Report

"Based on an analysis of actual investor behavior over the 20 years ending December 31, 2011, the average equity investor would have earned an annualized return of 3.49% underperforming the S&P by more than 4.3% and outpacing inflation by a mere 0.49%."

Quantitative Analysis of Investor Behavior (QAIB)

---

a scare tactic—that's being realistic.

And how long does it take to make your money back? Longer than you'd hope. Let's take a look at some examples in history. [11] After the Great Depression which lasted from 1929-32, the Dow fell 89% and took a full 22 years to recover, Now, 22 years until recovery isn't typical, so let's look at a few more recent drops.

In 1973-74, the Dow fell by approximately 45%. It didn't recover until December 1982. That's an 8-year gap before the investors were back in the black.

Of course we all immediately think of the crash of 2008. After the market peaked on October 9, 2007, stocks slid downward. By March 5, 2009, the S&P was down 56% and the Dow down 53%. This recovery was four years in the making.

Too many people have bought into Wall Street's claim

that it's necessary to take a risk on order to get returns. They like calculating how much money you'll have in retirement if you stick with them. But they're only talking about 8, 10 or even 12%—is that return rate enough to justify the risk? And as far as retirement goes, are they considering taxes and fees?

We all know people who've had their retirement wiped out by a turn in the market—years of planning erased with one swipe. In just one year during the great recession of 2008, the Dow Jones Industrial lost 1/3 of its value! And we're left with no recourse, no way to protect ourselves.

There's another issue to be addressed, and that's the market's claim that they can provide a 12-15% return in the first place. DALBAR Inc. (the nation's leading financial services market research firm) shows that the average investor outpaced inflation by just 0.49% over the past several years. That's a far cry from 12%, let alone 15%.

Conversations around the water cooler sometimes drift to discussions about the hottest new stocks out there, but let's look at some numbers.

Let's say that Joe starts with $10,000 and gets a 100% rate of return in year one, bouncing his balance up to $20,000.

The next year, the market drops by 50%, leaving him

"In a 2012 report on 401(k) fees, the Government Accountability Office (GAO) concluded that such charges (fees) could "significantly decrease retirement savings."

Government Accountability Office; www.gao.gov

Year	Market	Starting Balance	Ending Balance
1	+ 100%	10,000	20,000
2	- 50%	20,000	10,000
3	+ 100%	10,000	20,000
4	- 50%	20,000	10,000

with $10,000 again. In year three, it goes up again by 100% to $20,000, then drops again in the fourth year by 50%, setting him right back at $10,000.

In this case, the market did average a 25% rate of return. But how much additional cash does Joe have left to show for his 25% average rate of return?

Zero.

Even though brokers quote stats about great rates of return in the market, investors could still be netting absolutely zero.

Take that same $10,000, compound it for four years at 6.5% with no risk in the market, and you could end up with $12,960.20.

A 25% return in the market gave Joe $10,000, but a much lower 6.5% rate, compounded every year, would give him almost $13,000. It's easy to see why people are getting confused about where they should put their money.

Adding Insult to Injury

After the market has wiped out your principal, you're still socked with fees. Often, 401(k)s, mutual funds, and other stock-market-related investments come with fees that many people don't understand because they can be written in legalese and buried in the fine print.

Compounded over time, this 1-3% fee structure can mean the difference between security and just scraping by. Even if you do realize a 10% return in the market, it could end up being 7-8% after fees.

Even a 1% point difference in fees can have a big impact. Let's take a 35-year-old worker who leaves $20,000 in his 401(k) plan when he switches jobs and never adds to that account. If the account earned 7% a year, minus 0.5% in annual fees, his balance would only grow to about $132,000 at retirement. But if the fees were 1.5% annually, the average net return would be reduced to 5.5%, and the $20,000 would grow to about $100,000. Over 30 years, the 1% increase in fees whittled down the account balance by nearly 25%. [12] Even worse, when you tack on fees while you are losing money, it can be very difficult to regain the ground you've lost so you can start making progress again.

You Can't Harvest a Shrinking Crop

After losing so much money, Tom was determined to do things differently the second time around. He studied it out and decided what he really wanted. That included a way to save his money and prepare for retirement without unnecessary complications. He wanted a simple plan, one that guaranteed growth. And it also needed to provide good tax benefits, and he wanted to be able to access it at any time without incurring fees and penalties.

Tom was a dreamer, right? No such plan exists.

Or does it?

Tom's optimism was well rewarded. After some searching, he settled on the perfect solution for him. It wasn't a get-rich-quick scheme and it didn't promise to lay golden eggs. But it was secure, and that was the most important thing to Tom. He was fearful of making the wrong choice, as many of us are at first, but he really liked what he saw and feels confident that he's chosen the right course for him.

To Sum It Up

When you start down the Safe Money path, you'll give yourself permission—permission to toss out the old idea that the only way to become wealthy is to risk your hard-earned money, permission to grow wealthy while protecting against some of the other enemies of wealth.

There is good news. There is a solution. The pathway of Safe Money is simple and proven. Soon you will have a clear plan to replace the conventional wisdom that has failed many people, with a proven solution that can give you relief, hope and faith in your future. (In fact, you can grab your own personalized Safe Money blueprint on www.21stcenturyfinancialservices.com)

With this book, you will now have the blueprint you need to make the moves that can protect your life, family, and finances by creating a rock on which you can build a financial foundation that you can count on.

Section 2

A New World

"I must create a system, or be enslaved by another man's."
— William Blake

"Reasonable people adapt themselves to the world.
Unreasonable people attempt to adapt the world to themselves.
All progress, therefore, depends on unreasonable people."
— George Bernard Shaw

CHAPTER 3

INSTANT GRATIFICATION AND TAKING ADVICE FROM GURUS

"There are as many opinions as there are experts."
— Franklin D. Roosevelt

"Even when the experts all agree, they may well be mistaken."
— Bertrand Russell

Back in 2008, Jim Cramer of Mad Money CNBC proclaimed his absolute belief that Bear Stearns was solid. Eleven days later, Bear Sterns had dropped from $69.00 to $2.00. This will just show you how unpredictable the market is, and how no one, even the financial gurus, can predict what's going to happen.

Where do you get most of your financial information? A lot of people only know what they read in magazines or hear on the radio. The HR department at your work has probably suggested that you invest in the 401(k) program so you'll get matching funds. Are these just talking heads, or are they dispensing valuable advice?

Let's look at this for a minute. Did you know that the 401(k) and other qualified retirement programs are trillion-dollar businesses? By some estimates, there are between 7 and 11 trillion dollars in qualified plans. That's a lot of money to trust to Wall Street stockbrokers and their computer systems. Perhaps some of this advice we keep hearing to invest in 401(k) programs is a little skewed—sounds like there's a lot of money to be made in this line of work.

Does It Really Work for Them?

Even if you've never listened to her, you've probably heard of Suze Orman, perhaps one of the most famous financial gurus to hit the airwaves. Orman hosts her own show, has written a handful of bestsellers, and was named by *Time* magazine as one of the world's one hundred most influential people. She encourages viewers, listeners, and readers to buy term and invest the difference in mutual funds—"investing" which could also be interpreted as "risking".

But does she practice what she preaches?

When asked, she has estimated her liquid net worth at about $25 million, with an additional $7 million in houses. And just how does she invest her own personal wealth?

"I save it and build it in municipal bonds. I buy zero-coupon municipal bonds and all the bonds I buy are triple-A-rated, and insured so even if the city goes under, I get my money," Orman says.

She doesn't sound too keen on risk when it comes to her own wallet. Her plan sounds pretty safe compared to a lot of other schemes out there.

Does she invest in the stock market? "I have a million dollars in the stock market, because if I lose a million dollars, I don't personally care." Very few people are in her boat, where a million dollars could come and go and she wouldn't really care. The average person can't afford that kind of risk, and unless they can absorb a loss like that, maybe they shouldn't take a risk like that.

Another interesting piece of the puzzle is that Suze is sponsored by TD Ameritrade, which is a huge company that—just like its name sounds—makes money facilitating stock trades. Suze's face is synonymous with their brand. Could she have any ulterior motives for encouraging you to buy term and invest the difference?

Jim Cramer of CNBC's Mad Money also recommends that people head toward the stock market with their non-retirement funds, pointing them in directions he claims will pay them back nicely.

Does That Work?

Cramer suggested that his viewers buy CIT Group, saying it was primed for upside. Fewer than four weeks later, CIT filed bankruptcy. The Cheat Sheet's assessment? "This type of incredibly speculative advice is as radioactive to the general investing public as a post nuclear explosion site. . . . If "In Cramer You Trust", (like the CNBC commercials tell you to do), you are probably going to have lost over 90% of your investment by the open on Monday." [13]

Summing it all up, a report in Baron's stated that, "Cramer is wildly inconsistent, and the performance of individual picks varies widely. So widely, in fact, that it is impossible to know with confidence that any sample of Cramer's recommendations will enable you to outperform the market." [14]

Stories like these are not uncommon. We turn to financial gurus seeking advice on what to do with our money, and oftentimes, they are wrong. They often tell us to head to Wall Street and invest in 401(k)s, buying term and investing the difference, but people are losing millions of dollars following that advice. [15]

When our clients follow the Safe Money path, we teach them how to build their house on a solid foundation. Would you hire a contractor who wanted to start out your structure with a foundation of clay or sand? Of course not. You'd hire someone who used concrete. You'd do everything you could to ensure the safety of your family within that house. Shouldn't you also take great care to place a solid foundation beneath your financial future?

The Safe Money path helps create that solid foundation you can depend on regardless of market crashes and dips— we aren't subject to the roller coaster of Wall Street. Plus, we have many other living benefits. We'll talk about those shortly.

To Sum It Up

So far on our Safe Money path, we've covered three critical topics:

1. We've been told for years that Wall Street is the answer—it's time to try something new.

2. The stock market is risky, with no guarantee of any return or solidarity for your future.

3. Be careful when listening to advice and consider the source. What do they have to gain from advising you the way they do?

There's something else we need to factor in to the equation. Keep reading to learn more about it through the incredible story of Willie Sutton.

CHAPTER 4

WILLIE SUTTON
AND THE TAX MAN

"In this world nothing can be said to be certain,
except death and taxes."
— Benjamin Franklin

Chances are you've heard of Willie Sutton. But in case you haven't, here's his story.

Willie was an ordinary kid, the fourth of five children. He was born in Brooklyn on June 30, 1901. He went to school, but his head was filled with dreams of fame and fortune, and he left home and school after the eighth grade.

Taking a string of low-paying jobs like gardening, drilling, and clerking, he had enough for his basic needs, but he wanted more. He had a taste for nice clothes and wanted a flashy lifestyle. He jumped from job to job, never holding one down for longer than eighteen months. He was always hungering for more.

He got married when he was twenty-eight, but was divorced shortly thereafter. Turns out his wife didn't want to be married to a jailbird—he'd been arrested for bank robbery.

His jail sentence wasn't very long and soon he was right back at it. He'd finally found something that brought in the kind of cash he thought he deserved. He became a master of disguise, earning the nickname "The Actor". He dressed as a mailman and attempted to rob the Corn Exchange Bank and Trust Company in Philadelphia, Pennsylvania, but a passerby became suspicious and ruined everything for him. But less than a year later, he came back and was successful. Other disguises included a maintenance man and a police officer. Once he posed as a telegraph messenger and pulled off a very lucrative job at a Broadway jewelry store in broad daylight.

Willie wasn't mean and gruff like other bank robbers. He was actually pretty polite. Witnesses to his robberies reported that he was quite a gentleman. One even said that being robbed by Willie Sutton was like going to the movies, except the usher had a gun.

In June 1931, things took a downward turn for Willie. He was arrested, charged with assault and robbery, and was sentenced to 30 years in prison. But that didn't much matter—18 months later, Willie roped two nine-foot sections of ladder together and simply climbed over the prison wall.

On February 5, 1934, Willie brought a machine gun

with him to the Corn Exchange Bank and Trust Company. He was apprehended and sentenced to serve 25 to 50 years in the Eastern State Penitentiary in Philadelphia.

But Willie wasn't about to serve that sentence either. On April 3, 1945, he was one of 12 convicts who burrowed out of the penitentiary through a tunnel—his fifth escape attempt from the same prison. He was recaptured the same day. Now a fourth-time offender, he was tossed back in prison and transferred to the Philadelphia County Prison in Holmesburg, Pennsylvania. The officials thought he might have a harder time escaping from a new location.

Two years went by in Pennsylvania, but Willie wasn't finished. He and a group of other prisoners dressed up as prison guards and walked right across the grounds carrying ladders. When the prison search light focused in on them, Willie Sutton smiled and yelled, "It's okay," and kept moving with his plan. For some reason, no one questioned him. He was free again.

Three years after that escape, Willie was added to the FBI list of Ten Most Wanted Fugitives. The FBI took an unusual approach to apprehending him. Rather than just distributing his poster to police departments throughout the nation, they also gave his photograph to tailors. Willie did enjoy the finer things in life, a well-made suit being one of them. Two years later, Willie was riding the subway in New York City when a twenty-four-year-old tailor's son recognized him as the man from the wanted posters. He shadowed Willie to a gas station and called the police while watching Willie buy a battery for his car.

When the police arrived, Willie Sutton didn't resist arrest, but he didn't confess to anything, either. He was taken into Queens County Court and sentenced to an additional 30 years to life. It didn't make much difference—Willie already owed one life sentence plus 105 years. They threw him into a cell at Attica State Prison. He'd never be a free man again.

Of course, that wasn't the end of the story. It never is, with someone like Willie. Seventeen years later, Willie became seriously ill with emphysema and also needed major surgery on the arteries in both his legs. On Christmas Eve of 1969, the State of New York released Willie Sutton from prison. He was sixty-eight.

Strangely enough, two years later, Willie did a television commercial to promote the new photo credit card for a Connecticut bank. How's that for irony? He also authored two books about his escapades. When he was asked why he robbed banks, he said, "Because that's where the money is." [16]

Willie Sutton's Law

Willie robbed banks because that's where the money was. Wherever wealth is accumulated, someone will always try to take it. This is called by some, "Willie Sutton's Law".

You might feel you are living Willie Sutton's Law every day—many of us do. Between our everyday living expenses and debts and interest, it seems as though we're constantly being robbed.

Who is the modern-day Willie Sutton imposter? The tax man!

But how can we keep more of our money in our pockets? Here are some suggestions. The first has to do with paying taxes.

Of course we should all contribute to maintaining our great country. But did you know just how many taxes you could end up paying by investing in a qualified retirement plan? It's staggering. There's a way to keep that from happening to you.

Just What About Those Taxes?

You've been reading your paycheck stubs and you know that up to 20-30% of your income is going to taxes. This hardly seems fair—you've done all the work, and yet you don't get to keep all your income. Thomas Jefferson said that an income tax of even 1% is equivalent to slavery. What does that make 20-30%?

It's bad enough to give this much away in income tax, but that's not even skimming the surface. What about state income tax, social security tax, property tax, Medicare tax, phone tax, utility tax, sales tax, gasoline tax, and vehicle tax—not just on the purchase, but also on the annual registration? Sound familiar? You pay taxes with almost every move you make, from brushing your teeth to checking your e-mail. It can feel like the tax man is waiting for you in the shadows to rob you, just like Willie Sutton. It's just adding insult to injury when you have to pay even more taxes on the money you've saved for retirement.

The Trillion-dollar Tax Target

But what about tax-deferred programs set up by the government to help people invest for retirement? Isn't it great that we don't have to pay those taxes upfront? We may not be paying them upfront, but pay them we will, whether we want to or not.

Did you know that trillions of dollars are accumulated in government-sponsored qualified retirement plans like IRAs and 401(k)s?

The profits from those plans could end up lining Uncle Sam's pockets. Let me ask you a question. If you were a farmer, would you rather pay taxes on the corn seed or the corn harvest?

It's a very simple question. Would you rather pay for a bag of seed before you've put in all the hard work and diligent care, or would you rather pay taxes on truckload after truckload of grain from the harvest? Did you realize you had a choice?

In the government-sponsored, tax-deferred retirement plans, you pay taxes on all the increase. You're paying taxes on the truckloads of crops—at a time when you need that money the most. With the plan we'll show you, you pay taxes on the seed. The crops are yours, and you get to keep all the money you grow.

To help you more clearly understand how this works, let's look at some actual figures.

Option 1: The 7702 Plan™

Invest $5,000 a year for 30 years.

Total of $150,000.

In a 33% tax bracket, you pay $49,500 in taxes on that money as you earn it over the 30 years.

Assume you experience a 6.5% growth rate on that money. By the end of the 30 years, you'll have $348,854.18 in your account.

(Get your own personalized 7702 Plan ™ on
www.21stcenturyfinancialservices.com)

Option 2: A tax-deferred plan like a 401(k)

Invest $5,000 a year in the stock market for 30 years.

Growth rate: 6.5%

Total of $498,017.98.

You didn't pay taxes up front on this money, so at this point, you have more money. Looks pretty good, right?

But you can't forget Willie Sutton's Law—there's always someone waiting to take your wealth. How much of that money belongs to Uncle Sam? You have $498,017.98 in your retirement account. Let's say you take out $73,000 a year to live on during retirement. You can do that for nine years before your money is gone (assuming it's still growing at 6.5%). On that $73,000 each year, you now have to pay taxes on the "crop" (assuming you are in the same 33% tax bracket). Thus, you will pay $24,090 in taxes every year. In nine years, you will have paid $216,810 in taxes.

Remember how much you saved by deferring taxes—by waiting to pay on the crop instead of on the seed? You saved $49,500. That means you will have paid Uncle Sam back everything you saved in just the first two and a half years. In the next six and a half years, you will pay an additional $167,310 in taxes on your harvest.

In fact, according to Scott Shultz, you could end up paying up to five times more taxes using a qualified plan like a 401(k) than you saved during your entire working years. [17]

So, Mr. Farmer, what do you think—should you pay taxes on the seed or the crop?

You might believe that you'll be in a lower tax bracket when you retire, and it might make sense to defer your taxes for that reason. However, in later years, people often lose many of the deductions they presently have because kids have moved out and mortgages have been paid off.

In addition, there's no way to predict what the tax rates are going to be when you retire. How does the federal government plan to pay back the trillion-dollar deficit? Is there a plan in place right now? We can't say from one day to the next what the future will hold, but looking at the past shows that tax brackets have been as high as 92%.

As was mentioned a moment ago, you don't have to pay taxes on your crop. We'll show you how to beat Willie Sutton's Law by paying on your seed so you can enjoy what you reap. By paying on your seed, you are still meeting your tax obligation, but by doing it the way we'll show you, you won't be over-paying.

Paying tax on the seed gives you major tax advantages on your growth, while at the same time protecting the principal from risks in the market. You can have access to your money throughout your life, regardless of when you need it. It also allows you to transfer your wealth to your heirs without them having to pay income tax on that money.

To Sum It Up

The Safe Money path we're about to show you isn't just about keeping your money safe from market losses. It's about protecting your money from all the enemies of wealth, like taxes, market losses, and brokerage fees. In addition, it gives you leverage in your battle against another monster—the interest vampire.

CHAPTER 5

KILLING THE
INTEREST VAMPIRE

*"There are two types of people in the world.
Those who pay interest and those who EARN it."*
— Unknown

*"The rich rule over the poor,
and the borrower is servant to the lender."*
— Proverbs 22:7

*"Banks don't lend their money.
They lend the money somebody else left there."*
— Adam Smith

Most people spend a great deal of their time working to support their families, and yet, when their bills are paid, they are left with nothing extra to show for it. Many wonder if it's even worth it, if they will ever become free of the interest vampire sucking the life out of everything they do. These people become the financial living dead.

How would a 34% raise change your life?

That's how much you could be paying in interest on your after-tax income. That's like ripping a third off a twenty-dollar bill and handing it over to the tax man.

You might feel that you've done your due diligence by checking for good interest rates and keeping your credit score high. Those are two important areas of focus, but they're not the things that are killing you. You are being attacked and defeated by the volume of interest.

Imagine you go buy a car for $30,000 and get a five-year loan with an interest rate of 7.5%. How much will you pay in interest over the life of that loan? If you do the math on a calculator, you'll see that 7.5% of $30,000 is $2,250.

But that's not accurate.

You'll actually pay more than twice that much. The amount of interest you will pay on that $30,000 car loan could be up to $6,068.31—20.2% of the amount you borrowed.

This is because of three letters that follow your interest rate quote: APR, or annual percentage rate. The 7.5% is the rate you pay on the balance of the loan every

> **Safe Money Alert**
>
> Your 7.5% car loan could end up costing you more like 20.2% by the time you pay off that loan!

year. So by the time you are done paying off your car loan, you'll have paid over 20% on that loan, not just 7.5%.

Here's where the volume of interest comes in. Let's say, over the course of your lifetime, you finance 10 cars at $30,000 each. That's a total of $300,000. Assuming you get the same 7.5% interest on those loans, that means you'll pay about $6,000 in interest on each loan, or $60,000 in interest on your 10 cars. That's a big deal. A really big deal—especially when current figures reveal that the average American reaches retirement age with only $88,000 in savings. That means you will have dumped out, in interest on cars, almost as much as most people save for their entire retirement. And leasing can be even worse for your financial health.

> **Safe Money Alert**
>
> If you thought interest on cars was hard to swallow, this might really make you sick. Home loans are front-loaded with most of the interest paid in the first years of the loan. Because of how often people refinance homes, over 10 or 20 years of paying down mortgages, up to 86% of every dollar you pay on your mortgage could be going straight to interest!

With purchase price and interest combined on your 10 cars, even if you keep them until they're paid off, you will have spent $360,000 on your cars. That is four times what many people save for their retirement.

What difference would it make to your life if you could keep the majority of that $360,000 in YOUR pocket instead of going to some lender or car company?

Wouldn't your entire financial outlook be different?

There is a tool to help you achieve this.

To introduce you to this great financial tool, I want to tell you about one of my favorite movies, Déjà Vu, starring Denzel Washington.

At one point in the movie, Denzel faced an impossible task. He had to explain to the woman he was trying to save that he was from the future. It was vital to her survival that she know what was happening, so he asked her this critical question: "What if you had to tell someone the most important thing in the world, but you knew they wouldn't believe you?"

After thinking for a moment, she looked at him and replied, "I'd still try."

What if you could help people solve some of their biggest financial problems, but you were afraid no one would believe you?

Would you still try?

This incredible financial tool is considered ineffective or antiquated by the financial gurus who would seek to discredit it. Banks, stockbrokers, and mutual fund managers never promote it.

Why? Because it doesn't serve them—it serves you.

Financing Your Own Prosperity™

It seems that the system has been set up to make a few people rich while putting the thumbscrews on the average person. But by using a time-tested financial tool we call a 7702 Plan™, you can set yourself up to enjoy the cars, home improvement projects, and vacations you want—without paying interest to a bank or credit card company. Plus, you get to recoup your principal and put it back into your plan rather than losing it forever when you make a purchase.

Here's how Financing Your Own Prosperity™ works:

1. First, you accumulate cash value into a 7702 Plan™.

2. When you are ready to buy your next car, go on vacation, or make any other major purchase, you borrow against your cash value. No credit check, no applications, no getting declined. Now you can make that purchase with cash.

3. Now, instead of paying a bank or credit card company, you pay yourself back. If you choose to pay extra interest, it will only increase your own cash value.

The Really Exciting Part

When you Finance Your Own Prosperity™ with a 7702 Plan™, the cash value continues to grow as if you've never touched the money.

That's right. You can take $30,000 out for a new car and your money continues to grow with the same guaranteed rate, as if it was never touched.

This may sound too good to be true, but it's real. We'll show you how it works in a moment.

The 7702 Plan™ is simple, secure, and guaranteed. It's built using a special type of cash value life insurance policy.

That's right—life insurance.

We've all been given a bad impression of life insurance, and it's not surprising if you're feeling a little squeamish right now. I never believed in cash value life insurance because for years, I had bought into the "buy term and invest the difference" hype from the financial gurus.

We've already discussed why investing the difference may not work out very well—there are so many taxes, fees, and market dips. And far too many people spend the difference rather than investing it.

Suze Orman and Dave Ramsey may have given the impression that life insurance is not a good investment. That's why it's important to use a 7702 Plan™, a modified cash value life insurance policy that allows you to grow the cash value as quickly as possible (in some cases up to 3-5 times faster than traditional life insurance policies), while putting as little money as possible toward insurance costs.

To Sum It Up

Take a look at some of the benefits you could get from a 7702 Plan™:

- Safe, guaranteed growth every year

- A time-tested financial product that has been stable for more than 100 years

- Largely untouched by major market crashes

- Guaranteed growth and principal

- Tax-advantaged growth (You can access your money without a taxable event!)

- Flexible financial tool allowing you to access money for major purchases, college funding, or other needs. (And most importantly for this chapter, it could allow you to Finance Your Own Prosperity™.)

Now that you understand the benefits a 7702 Plan™ could bring, let's see them in action.

SECTION 3

CREATING A SAFE MONEY FOUNDATION

"Do you wish to rise?
Begin by descending.
You plan a tower that will pierce the clouds?
Lay first the foundation."
— St. Augustine

CHAPTER 6

DEFEATING THE ENEMIES
OF WEALTH

*"Wherever wealth is accumulated,
someone will be there to try and steal it."*
— R. Nelson Nash

Jason Smith slid into the front seat, slammed the door, and slumped forward until his forehead pressed against the steering wheel. His stomach was in knots and a dull ache throbbed behind his temples. Another roller coaster week in the market had dropped his 401(k) value substantially.

He dreaded facing Susan. After all, it had been *his* idea to max out the 401(k). She'd wanted to keep their contributions smaller—to put some of Jason's salary in a conventional savings account or maybe some short-term CDs. She worried about emergencies and about covering the kids' college expenses—all arguments that he disregarded at the time.

He'd read some articles written by the industry's top gurus, and he figured he knew what he was doing. He knew that the 401(k) was the most popular retirement plan in America. He not only wanted all the free money he could get through his employer's match, but he'd heard about the great tax savings to be had from socking the maximum amount possible into a 401(k). All the other guys in his department were doing it and they seemed savvy enough.

Jason had won out, and for the past six years a large percentage of every paycheck had gone to his 401(k) account. It had seemed like a good idea at the time. But that was *before.*

Before the market experienced a nearly unprecedented crash that slashed the value of mutual funds and crushed retirement accounts of people all over the country.

Before he'd found out—how had he not known this?— that the money in his 401(k) might as well have been locked up in Fort Knox because it was a major pain to get at any of it. After all, it was *his* money. And he needed some of it. And now—easing reluctantly up the driveway—Jason knew that what had seemed like such a good idea six years ago was turning out to be an emotional and financial roller coaster with more downs than ups.

Jason sank onto the sofa in the living room and proceeded to tell Susan the bad news. Another drop in economic forecasts had caused a major drop in the market, which was costing them thousands with every drop. First off, his account was not even worth *half* of what he thought it was. His hard-earned money was gone, thanks to the plunge of a market over which he had no control.

So much for his plan of retiring with millions like he'd dreamed about.

Second, Susan had really wanted to access some money for the kitchen remodel they badly needed. If he took the money out, he'd be slapped with so many fees and penalties—including an enormous tax penalty—that he'd scarcely even break even.

Even if he decided to brave the penalties, he'd lose a fortune selling the funds in his account when the market was so low. He would kiss away what hadn't already been lost to the market crash.

Finally, he didn't even dare borrow from his account. The little carrot that had been dangled in front of his nose six years ago turned out to have a very painful string attached.

What they hadn't told Jason when he invested in a 401(k) was that if he lost his job, the loan would be due in full, usually within two months' time.

With a rumored corporate merger in the works that could result in potential layoffs, that was a chance Jason couldn't afford to take.

Maxing out the 401(k)—not the best idea, Jason sheepishly admitted.

A few days later, after some emails between friends, Jason got a link to an online site that could compute his True Financial Age. He was intrigued.

It would tell him his "Never Work Again" number. He started punching in numbers, thinking things couldn't possibly get worse, and while he was a bit shocked at what he saw, he also got some good news.

Jason Smith, at age 42, had a True Financial Age of 81.

Simply put, here's what that means: In order to have enough money put away for retirement, Jason would have to work until he was 81 years old.

Eighty-one? Jason wasn't sure he'd even *live* that long! As visions of greeting customers at the local warehouse store clouded his thoughts, he noticed that the website offered a way out—and it could all be explained by a Safe Money Associate. ™ Let's just say it was a hard sell for Susan. We can imagine why she might be just a little skeptical about Jason's financial know-how right about now.

Reluctantly, Susan agreed, and Jason filled out the request online to meet with an SMA, Michael, who said he could help them get on the Safe Money path while kissing the stock market roller coaster good-bye.

It was done using a 100-year-old proven way to keep your money safe. It came with guaranteed growth each year, a way to potentially experience the ups of the markets without the downs . . . and could give you the ability to access your cash value throughout your life. In fact, that was one of the major benefits of the plan—that you could use it to Finance Your Own Prosperity™. This meant you could borrow against your plan for major purchases like cars, college tuition, or vacations and then pay your loan back to yourself while the cash continued to grow as if you hadn't touched it. Jason was particularly intrigued by that idea. Ultimately, it was a way to possibly reduce the amount of interest you would pay to banks or credit card companies!

Let's take a break in the story while we're waiting for Michael to show up and get a few of the basics out of the way. Because whether you have a 401(k) or not, this will be a new information. And like GI Joe says, "Knowing is half the battle."

You might have assumed, just like our friend Jason, that a 401(k) or mutual fund is a solid way to save for retirement. After all, that's what many of the pop culture gurus advocate. Right out of the gate, let's see what one financial analyst had to say about it:

> The American public has been hoodwinked by political and corporate forces into relying on the 401(k) as the primary long-term investment mechanism. In doing so, the stock market has been put at center stage in providing for a comfortable retirement for the average American. The 401(k) represents an implicit promise to middle-class Americans that they can live off the income that they receive from stock ownership, just like the rich do. It is a promise impossible to fulfill; it is the great 401(k) hoax. [18]

"Hoax" sounds like a pretty strong word, but that's potentially what the 401(k) plan is.

Here's a quick crash course on 401(k) plans. Money in 401(k) plans is often invested in stocks and mutual funds. If the market goes up, so can your money. If you have money in a 401 (k) with stocks or mutual funds, your money could be at risk for loss!

That means if the market goes down, you can lose. Lastly, your 401(k) contributions are made *before* you pay taxes on the money, so you're taxed as you withdraw money from the plan. (Here's where you see that you are being taxed on the crop, not the seed.) And don't forget, your money could be tied up until you retire, unless you want to pay the penalties and taxes on an early withdrawal.

Now, let's get back to the meeting with Michael.

It's seven o'clock on Thursday evening, and Michael, Jason, and Susan are sitting around the kitchen table. Jason is all ears. But Susan, feeling like she's just had the proverbial blanket yanked out from under her feet with the 401(k) debacle, is hanging back. Susan, still skeptical, goes for the jugular with this comment:

"I need to ask something right up front," she says. Michael welcomes the question. After detailing what had just happened with their 401(k), Susan squares herself up in her chair. "We've listened to other financial gurus and advisors and it's gotten us where we are now. Why should we listen to you?"

"I understand your skepticism in talking with another financial advisor. The difference is, I'm focused on Safe Money. I help people build a strong foundation of safety so they never lose money in the market downturns. 401(k) plans or mutual funds can be the *risky* kind of investing," Michael explains. "In fact, depending on how you direct your contributions, it could put all of your retirement principal at risk." Susan, clearly frustrated, glares at Jason.

"Tonight I'm going to talk to you about some of the biggest enemies of building wealth and also about how you can start on the Safe Money path to retirement.

"A couple of the threats that we must protect against to have a Safe Money retirement are 1) the actual loss of your money in the market (once you lose money, it can take a substantial amount of time to make it up), 2) taxes, and 3) interest. Many folks don't know it, but they could be paying up to one-third of every dollar they make toward interest of some sort. This is essentially making them employees of the tax man and the lenders at the same time.

"Let's talk about putting your money at risk of loss. To begin, let's look at how your mutual fund or stock performs. How much money you end up with for retirement usually depends completely on the market," Michael explains. "The market is uncertain, risky, and completely out of your control. So your future is tied to how well the market cooperates, without any input from you."

While Jason and Susan tried to wrap their heads around that piece of information, Michael started asking some pretty tough questions. "Jason, how much do you really know about your 401(k)?"

"Clearly not as much as I thought I did," Jason mumbles.

"Well, let's start with your 401(k) manager—do you even know who it is?" Jason shakes his head, and Michael goes on. "Do you know what funds you're invested in or even what companies your funds invest in? Most people enrolled in 401(k) plans can't even list the funds or companies in which they are investing. That's risky business."

"Interesting," Susan smugly replies. "That sounds more like *gambling* to me."

"There's more," Michael says. "I know that you've already found out about some of the tax implications. Think about this: If you don't like paying taxes right now, what makes you think you're going to like it any better 20 years from now? When you start to withdraw your 401(k) money for retirement, you're going to have to pay taxes on it. That means if you're in a 28% tax bracket, you could have about one-third less actual money than you have in your account."

(A quick point: in a 401(k) plan, you'll be paying taxes on the crop, not the seed. And this is called tax savings? What an irony. People invest in a 401(k) plan to save taxes, but in reality, they could end up actually paying *more* taxes—not only because they're paying on the crop, but because they could potentially be in a higher tax bracket when they begin taking distributions from their 401(k) plans.)

"You've got three children, right?" Michael asks. Susan nods. "If you don't manage to use up your 401(k) during your retirement, it will be passed on to your heirs. Not only could they face income tax on the money they receive from your 401(k), but they could have to pay estate taxes as well. If you have more than $1 million in your estate, it could amount to 55%.

"There's another issue with a 401(k) plan you need to be aware of—fees. Many folks don't know how much in fees they are really paying. Unfortunately, it can add up to a substantial sum, and the fund managers always get paid whether your money grows or not."

Jason slaps his palm against the table. "I feel like I've been misled. Our HR guy pushed a bunch of papers in front of me and encouraged me to sign on the dotted line, all the while touting matching funds and company support. But he never said anything about getting out! All the gurus on TV, and everyone else for that matter, say to max out my 401(k)."

Susan clears her throat loudly.

"Oh, yeah, well—everyone except Susan," Jason admits.

Now both Jason and Susan are now ready to listen to Michael. He's shown them why the old way wasn't working. Jason feels like he's learned more about the 401(k) program in the last 20 minutes than in the previous two decades.

Susan, who has softened a little toward Jason, says, "I'm feeling ripped off too. Just yesterday, I read a column by a well-respected financial guru. Her advice was to buy term and invest the difference in mutual funds. It's ironic that she was the spokesperson for TD Ameritrade who probably makes millions off people who invest in the market through their system."

How efficient do you think the average business would be if it suffered constant turnover—in other words, if new people came in on a regular basis, bringing new ideas and new ways of doing things? Well, that's what happens with mutual funds—except instead of people, the turnover involves stocks (in other words, excessive trading in the portfolio). Mutual fund managers are constantly changing the stocks in the portfolio. (Translation: you never know from one day to the next exactly *what's* in your portfolio.)

In the 1950s, the average portfolio turnover rate was about 15%. Today, 100% turnover is commonplace, and as much as 300% turnover is typical. Just a few years ago, *Forbes* magazine reported turnover rates so high that even the reporter was astonished. Rates ranged from 523% to a staggering 827%. The result of all these turnovers is that the cost of doing business for mutual funds, instead of going down, has doubled since the 1950s. And who pays for the increased cost? That's right: the investors. Lucky dogs. [19]

Jason chuckles. "Yeah, we've both seen the results of those."

"We all watched as the market toppled," says Michael, "taking with it the retirement dreams of millions of Americans. Even those who had enjoyed growth watched as their nest eggs were crushed to nearly half their previous value. And they were powerless to do anything about it. But you know what?" Michael continues. "Even without the disastrous crash we recently witnessed, there are always ups and downs that we can't control. Studies have shown that over the past 180 years, the average market return after factoring for inflation is as low as 1.2%. [20]

"Here's what it amounts to," Michael says. "As an investor, you put up 100% of the money, and you take 100% of the risk. *You're* the one whose principal is on the line. This is fine if you have money you can stand to lose, but this is *not* the way that Safe Money retirees live. They build a solid foundation and protect the principal. You guys got started on the right foot by visiting our site, www.21stcenturyfinancialservices.com, right?"

"Yeah, I found your site because a friend referred me to it. I took the Safe Money Quiz, and it was really eye-opening. I felt like it was time to try a different approach."

Susan interjects, "The Safe Money program sounds good to me."

"It does make sense," Jason agrees. "But I'm not sure what to do at this point. I'm stuck in a crummy 401(k) I can't get out of, and I'm not thinking I can afford any mutual funds for a while— at least not until we pull out of the hole we're in. So, what do we do now?"

Michael smiles again and starts spreading out his papers. "Jason, I've got great news for you."

"It's about time I got some *good* news for a change!" Jason laughs.

"You're a whole lot better informed than when I got here," Michael points out. "And now I'm going to show you how you *can* get on the right track, starting today. Regardless of your situation with the 401(k), I think we'll find some good solutions together. I'm going to show you a plan that will keep your money safely out of the market, is guaranteed to grow every year, and offers a smart tax strategy that allows *you* to Finance Your Own Prosperity™. You could reduce or totally eliminate the amount you pay in interest to banks and credit card companies, plus, have access to your cash value throughout your life. It's called the 7702 Plan™. And it's a plan you can start right away. Sound good?"

Jason feels like he's about to cry again—this time from relief.

CHAPTER 7

FINANCE YOUR OWN PROSPERITY™

*"All truths are easy to understand once they are discovered;
the point is to discover them."*
— Galileo

"In very simple terms," Michael explains, "the 7702 Plan™ is a customized cash value life insurance policy. In the next few minutes, I'm going to show you how it's not only a protection plan, but a powerful Safe Money plan."

"Oh, no!" Susan cries. "Hold on. I've heard both Suze Orman and Dave Ramsey say that it's a bad idea to buy cash value life insurance."

"Yeah," Jason chimes in. "My buddy who's a CPA says cash value life insurance is the wrong way to go. Lots of the financial pieces I've studied paint a poor picture of it too. They say it's just too expensive."

"I'm going to debunk those myths for you in just a few minutes," Michael says, "and you're going to see how cash value life insurance—*if* it's structured properly—can be a very solid solution for building wealth."

"Better than term insurance?" Jason asks.

"It's in a different league than term insurance," Michael says. "Term insurance is important for one reason: to provide for your family in the event of an untimely death. It's a bit like renting, really. You rent the insurance for a set period of years, and after that term of 10 or 20 years is up, your insurance is gone. There's usually no equity in term policies. However, if you do happen to die during those years, your beneficiaries receive the death benefit from your policy."

Michael continues, "We, as Americans, spend more money insuring our cars than we do our lives. In fact, we actually do things in reverse: We focus on protecting the golden eggs—cars, homes, and other possessions—instead of protecting the goose that lays those golden eggs."

"I have to admit I'm guilty of that," Jason murmurs. "Pretty much all I've got is my little policy through work—a term policy—but, man, I sure shell it out on insurance for the cars and the house."

Michael nods in understanding. "A 7702 Plan™, using cash value insurance, can provide death benefit protection like term, but it also provides you with a safe place for your money. It's also sometimes referred to as *permanent* life insurance. And it's just what its name implies, too: it covers you until you die, as long as you keep the policy in force. While we've all watched the stock market rise and fall, with banks and companies failing, the insurance industry has stayed solid. Did you know that during the Great Depression, while the banks and Wall Street crashed, the insurance industry not only maintained its strength, but kept its promises? During the Great Depression, clearly the greatest period of economic stress to date in the nation's history, policyholder cash values in life insurance companies were safe. Contrast that with the estimated 9,000-10,000 banks that failed during that time [21] and again in 2010, when over 143 banks failed." [22]

"Wow, I had no idea," Jason says.

"I like to look at history," Michael explains. "From the early 1930s until about 1980, life insurance companies—not Wall Street—were the dominant architects, builders, and custodians of the nation's savings and retirement systems." [23]

Jason splits the air with a low whistle. "I'm surprised—I really am. I didn't know any of that. But here's my question: my current policy, as I said, is term life. I've looked at prices, and, quite frankly, term is less money each month."

"Well, remember the reason we're here—it's not just to talk insurance. It's to show you how you can build a Safe Money retirement," Michael explains. "A term life policy usually doesn't provide any benefits to you while you're living. A permanent cash value life policy provides quite a few significant benefits to you while you're still alive. A term life policy typically doesn't build any cash value; whereas a permanent cash value life policy is designed to do exactly that."

"So why isn't everybody doing this?" Susan asks. "If cash value is so good, why haven't I heard more about it?"

SAFE MONEY - BRENT TYCKSEN & TERRY KEYZER

"That's a very good question," Michael says. "As good as cash value insurance is, it's important to realize that not all cash value policies work the same way. The criticisms targeted at permanent insurance often revolve around the fact that agents make large commissions on traditional policies. Also, too much of your money or yearly premiums go to buy insurance, instead of building cash value.

"For the 7702 Plan™, we've chosen companies that will allow you to max-fund the cash value side of the plan. Typically, this means that you can put as much money as possible toward your cash value and as little as possible toward the actual insurance costs.

"The vast majority of financial professionals and insurance agents don't know how to do this properly to maximize your cash value growth. They've never been trained. You certainly don't get this advanced training when you study for your license! That's what makes working with me, a Safe Money Associate, different—our specialty is to maximize your cash growth, not your insurance costs. Going this route typically cuts an agent's commission in about half, but I gladly do it because it's better for my clients. Many agents don't see it this way— they'd rather double up the commission at the cost of the client. That is *not* how we do things.

"The secret is not only working with a professional like me who understands how to build the policy correctly, but also in working with companies who support the concept," Michael explains.

Again, let's step back a moment from the story and review the key ingredients for building a 7702 Plan™. Here are a few of the most important pieces:

1. You want an insurance company with a long history of success and financial stability. One of the companies we work with has been in business for over 300 years and actually insured the home that Isaac Newton lived in.

2. You need an advisor who has been trained to create maximum cash value growth without hurting your tax advantages.

3. You need a company that will allow you to maximize cash value growth while minimizing your insurance costs. This is critical!

4. When you take a loan, your money can continue to grow as though you've never borrowed against your policy.

"Basically, here's what happens," Michael explains. "You buy a properly structured cash value life policy that you agree to pay into each month. You are contractually promised a guaranteed amount of growth every year—even if you borrow from it and even when you take an income from it during retirement. You've got a predictable financial vehicle: It's guaranteed for life, and your principal is guaranteed, so you won't lose it during market swings. And you get what we call 'living benefits' from a 7702 Plan™"

There are actually several other Safe Money options you can use, depending on your situation and your goals. There are also Income for Life Safe Money Plans that can guarantee you never outlive your money. This can mean great peace of mind for folks going into retirement. There are also what we call 'super-charged' 7702 Plans™ that allow you to experience the ups of market growth without the risk. This

Let's say you buy the finest-quality chocolate bar available (representing term life insurance). You love chocolate and would like nothing more than to sink your teeth into that bar, but the people from whom you bought it say you can't do that. By law, you have to put it away. You can't touch it. It won't go to waste, though. As soon as you die, your heirs get to savor that chocolate bar on the way home from your funeral.

Who wants to buy a chocolate bar they can't even enjoy? You sure wouldn't want to pay much for it, would you? That's why term life is so popular: it costs less. In fact, it's the smallest amount of money you can invest and still provide *some* money for your heirs. But take a look at the reason it costs so much less—it's only in effect for a specified length of time, and it provides benefits only to your heirs. There's no benefit to you.

Okay, back to the chocolate bar metaphor. Now, say you buy the finest-quality chocolate bar available (representing cash value life insurance). This time, though, you're able to savor that chocolate bar while you're still alive. In fact, your chocolate bar keeps getting bigger and bigger—so not only do you get to *keep* enjoying it, but when you die, your heirs will have even more chocolate to enjoy together. And while they're enjoying the smooth sweetness, they'll do so with the satisfaction of knowing you enjoyed it too.

is really exciting, and we'll cover it in a subsequent chapter.

Just go to www.21stcenturyfinancialservices.com to get a free analysis from a Safe Money Associate of what type of Safe Money plan will be right for you.

From here on, when we—and Michael—talk about cash value insurance, we're talking about the kind of 7702 Plan™ that provides these powerful benefits to you—

offered by the kind of companies we work with. Just about anyone can use it (you don't need to be educated or experienced) and it can work on autopilot (you don't have to watch the market, reassess stocks based on performance, or worry about tax consequences). And while it requires a bit of patience, it can work whether you have thousands or just a few hundred to contribute.

Now, let's get back to the story.

"So far it's sounding pretty good," says Susan, "but what do you mean by *living benefits?*"

"I've already mentioned a few," Michael responds. "The 7702 Plan™ gives you growth that is guaranteed by the insurance company to accumulate cash while being immune from whatever the stock market is doing. Another benefit is taxes. The IRA expert Ed Slott says, 'Life insurance is the single biggest benefit to the IRS tax code.' [24] You save taxes on the growth of your principal, you can access the cash value without paying taxes, and when the death benefit is paid out to your heirs, it comes to them income-tax free in most cases because you paid taxes on the money before you put it into your policy.

"And remember that one of the risks of 401(k) plans and mutual funds is the risk that the government could change the rules midstream due to the latest political agenda or bureaucratic whim," Michael says. "With a 7702 Plan™, your policy is a private contract between you and the insurance company.

"Of course, one of the greatest living benefits is your ability to reduce or totally stop paying interest to banks and Finance Your Own Prosperity™," Michael explains.

"How does that work?" Jason asks.

"We'll use a car for example. Let's say you want to buy a $20,000 car. You can get a loan from a bank or car financing company, or in your case, use your 7702 Plan™ to finance the car.

"With traditional car financing, you might finance the car for five years or so. In the end, you have a car paid off and you've lost all the interest and principal to the finance company. When you Finance Your Own Prosperity™, you take the cash out of your 7702 Plan™ and pay for the car in cash. (Often, paying cash can save you money on the purchase price by itself.) Then you make payments back to your policy. This is where it gets exciting—after the five years, you've got your car paid off, but you also have the $20,000 back into your own 7702 Plan™!

"Plus, you can pay additional interest on your payments and the extra money will go to increase your cash value. This is why we call it Finance Your Own Prosperity™, because each time you take out a loan and pay it back with extra interest, it actually increases your cash value."

"That sounds interesting!" Susan says.

"With a cash value insurance policy," Michael continues, "you have access to the cash value in your policy, and you can't be turned down for a loan. If you need to borrow the cash value from your policy, just say the word. No credit check, no tax returns, no qualifying hassle. And no one is going to raise your interest rate if you're late on a payment. In fact, *you* determine the repayment timetable, and *you* decide how often and for how long you want to make payments."

"This almost sounds too good to be true," Jason says.

"It gets even better," Michael responds. "Remember when we talked about how one of the enemies of wealth is interest? When you use your 7702 Plan™ to finance your purchases, your money continues to grow at the same guaranteed rate, as though you never touched a dime. When you pay the loan back, you recoup the cost of that purchase back into your policy, rather than making payments to someone else. You can enjoy some of the things you'd like without destroying your nest egg."

By this time, Jason and Susan are both wide-eyed. "There's got to be a hitch," Susan says, "and I can think of a big one. I'm not sure we'd even qualify for insurance right now. I just had some really serious health problems."

"If you're too old or have health issues that might make you uninsurable, you're not out of luck," Michael explains. "You can buy a policy on a child, spouse, or grandchild who does qualify to be insured. You own the policy, and you still control it so you decide what happens to the money. So let's assume you can qualify. If your policy is structured properly, your policy is permanent. That means as long as you keep it in force, it will be with you forever. This is extremely important when it comes to taxes. Life insurance is one of the best estate-tax planning vehicles there is because it gets paid to your estate income tax free."

Michael adds, "That's another one of the great benefits: your life is insured. The average man in this country has an economic value of more than $1 million dollars. If you die, especially if you die early, your family could suffer a significant economic loss on top of the emotional sorrow of losing you. Insurance provides financially for those you leave behind. In fact, as long as it's in force, your policy will generally pay out a lump-sum income-tax-free death benefit that's far larger than the total contributions you made to your plan.

"Now keep in mind, as we're referencing Finance Your Own Prosperity™, we're talking about policy loans, not withdrawals. Withdrawals are when you permanently take the money out of the policy. We use loans because your money continues to grow even while you are using it. Then, as you pay it back, it is there for you to use again and again.

"The idea is to be able to structure the loans so they can be paid back, similar to a regular car loan. If, for some reason, you can't make payments for a while, it's not a huge deal. No one will be knocking on your door to collect. You simply resume paying when you can. However, you definitely want to pay the loans back if you are using them to Finance Your Own Prosperity™."

"But what happens if we can't, for some reason?" Susan asks.

"You will continue to pay interest on the loan, and ultimately the policy could cancel. Just like gardening—if you stop watering a plant, it stops growing. We want to keep nurturing the 7702 Plan™ so it continues to grow. Then, once you hit your retirement years, we can structure your policy so it is paid up and you never have to pay more into it. It can then be there to provide retirement income.

"But," Michael says, "here's the real beauty of a loan from your plan: *you* structure the repayment schedule. *You* determine how much you can pay and how often you want to pay."

"Makes sense, but is there a limit to how much we can contribute?" Jason asks.

"Yes," Michael says. "We want to make sure that your plan doesn't become a Modified Endowment Contract (MEC). In order to enjoy the maximum tax benefits of your 7702 Plan™, you want to keep the policy within the MEC limit. The IRS has set up guidelines that dictate how much cash value you can put into a policy compared to the insurance amount. If you exceed their limits, meaning you put in too much cash, it could have negative tax implications—essentially ruining one of the major benefits for getting a 7702 Plan™. As Safe Money Associates, we are trained on how to structure the 7702 Plan™ so you stay under the MEC limit to enjoy maximum tax advantages."

"Yeah," Jason replies, "I can see why we want to work with someone who's been trained to do this properly. I'd hate to lose out on tax savings just because of an untrained advisor."

"If this is so great," Susan chimes in, "why haven't I heard anything about it? Is it because it's new?"

"Absolutely not," Michael answers. "In fact, Americans have been using 7702 Plan™-type permanent life insurance policies for over 100 years. Large companies, business people, and average citizens protect their capital by buying cash value life insurance policies on their employees and then using these cash value life insurance policies as safe money foundations. One reason why you might not have heard about it is that gurus, bankers, and Wall Street have no interest in promoting 7702 Plans™ because they often want you to invest in the market."

"Okay." Jason nods. "So how do we get started?"

"The bottom line is this," Michael explains. "You can start funding a 7702 Plan™ using a special type of cash value insurance life policy. Then, instead of borrowing from a bank, you borrow from your policy. You simply use a different way to pay for things—a method that lets you recoup the cost of large purchases, instead of letting that money go into a lender's pocket. And all the while you're growing a tidy nest egg, one you can predict and, even better, one you can count on."

"That *sounds* good," Susan agrees, "but I'm not sure I understand. Why not just put my money in an interest-bearing savings account and then use that money to buy the things I want? Wouldn't I actually come out ahead in the long run?"

"First," Michael replies, "how much does your money grow in a bank account while you aren't using it for something else? 1.5 - 2%, if you are lucky? If you invest in a bond or CD, the percentage of growth will be a little higher. Now consider this: with a 7702 Plan™, not only can your money grow at a guaranteed rate, but if you structure it right—and as a professional, I know how to do it right—you could also receive growth when the market goes up without risking your money in the market.

"But here's the part of the answer that's really convincing," Michael continues. "Let's say you deposit your money in a bank account, and then withdraw the $20,000 we talked about to pay cash for a car. Does the bank continue to pay you interest on the money you withdrew? Of course not. But guess what? Your 7702 Plan™ policy *does*. That's the amazing thing about a 7702

Plan™. People really think it's too good to be true, yet it is true, and it can be a great financial tool for those who take advantage of it."

"I've got to admit, I'm pretty stunned by all this," Jason says. "I just went through a pretty big hassle with the 401 (k) deal—are there rules here? I mean, what kinds of things can I borrow money for?"

"You can borrow from your account for anything you want," Michael answers. "You can run many of your large purchases through it—cars, vacations, business expenses, home improvement, and even real estate purchases. It's your money, and no one is going to tell you what you can do with it."

"So, it's like our own source of financing," Susan says. "But we set the terms and have more control over it."

"Exactly," says Michael. "In the end, what your 7702 Plan™ really can give you is a plan you can count on, a foundation for your financial plan without risking your principal or worrying about what the market is doing, or getting access to your money if something comes up. It's a predictable and safe way to put away your money. Following this plan could ultimately create millions of dollars in wealth for you and your family, while at the same time allowing you to reduce the amount of interest you are paying to banks."

The relief on Jason's face is obvious. "After what we've been through, this would really allow me to sleep well at night," he says.

"Absolutely." Michael responds. "You don't even have to wait until you retire. You get to enjoy the benefits now.

For example, if you want to take a family vacation next year, just get started now. When the time comes, you pull out a couple thousand dollars and go. Then pay the loan back and you recoup the cost of that vacation and it's there for you when you need it next time."

"So we can use it for the kitchen remodel we're thinking of doing too, huh?" says Susan.

"Absolutely," Michael replies. "Home improvement, college, cars, even investing in a business or real estate—whatever you want. Then, when you're ready to retire, you can take withdrawals and loans without having to pay taxes on that money as long as it is structured properly."

"I'm pretty much sold," Jason says, and Susan nods. "But as you can imagine, we don't have a lot of cash on hand right now. How much do we have to invest to get started?"

"The cost to you is only the amount you want to pay in premiums," Michael says. "There are several different ways to get started. Some folks roll over their current 401(k) plans, some move part of their savings over—in fact, there are many different ways to find money to fund a 7702 Plan™. There's no determined amount you have to start with."

"But we have to make monthly premium payments, right?" asks Susan.

"Not necessarily," says Michael. "It's very flexible. You could pay all up front, pay yearly, or even set up what I call an 'automatic Safe Money machine'. This would automatically transfer money from your bank account and pay your premiums each month without you worrying about it. But I imagine the real question you were trying to ask is how you're going to come up with the extra money. That's something specific I want to talk over with you. There are quite a few places I can help you find money to fund your plan. I'm confident that you can easily—and probably painlessly—divert money from other sources to build your plan without changing your lifestyle. Let's start with the most obvious: how much money do you get back on tax returns each year?"

Jason says, "About $4,000 - $5,000."

"Okay, so that's about $400 extra dollars every month you are sending to the IRS for no reason. Is there a reason you like to let Uncle Sam use your money for 12 months without paying you a dime of interest on it?"

"Well, when you put it like that, no, I guess it's not a good idea, is it? I just don't want to have to pay extra when the tax time comes around," Jason finishes.

"I understand. It's easy to set your deductions so that you still get a small refund while allowing most of your money to stay with you to use throughout the year. If you add up the $4,000 - $5,000 for the next 15-20 years of your working life, that could be an extra $100,000 you could put into your plan."

"Well, sheesh," Susan breaks in, "We should do that immediately!"

"We can build a plan that works for you. One client bought cash value policies on each of his boys when they were very young. At the time, his intention was to accumulate some cash, but to also provide them with death benefit coverage when they became adults and responsible for their individual families. As it turns out, one is now married with one daughter. He has cash value that can be used for his daughter's college expenses, braces, family vacations, or new cars. The young son, who is still single, has cash value to continue his college degree, replace his vehicle when the time comes, or make a down payment on a home."

"So we could set these up for our kids as well?" Susan asks.

"Yes. In fact, once they get their own plan in place, many people end up with multiple plans in the family. Kids can use them for college funding options, or to pay for their first car or house," Michael replies.

"So, once we get started, can we start using the money right away, or do we have to wait?" Jason asks.

"Usually you can access your cash value within a couple weeks. You could use it right away to fund that remodeling project you've been talking about.

"It's important to realize that a 7702 Plan™ is not a get-rich-quick scheme," emphasizes Michael. "It's a long-term plan to put you on the path to being able to retire with Safe Money. It requires diligence and patience."

"If by using your plan, we were able to cut back on some of the areas we're currently wasting, changing my withholdings so I keep more of my tax money throughout the year, and redirecting my $550 per month 401(k) contributions, that's about $400 per month on taxes, $550 on our current 401(k), and we're wasting another $50 per month right now on an extra landline phone we don't use. So how much could we have if we contributed about $1000 per month into a policy?" Jason asks.

How to Find Money to Fund a 7702 Plan™

1. I'll have that back, thank you. How much is your tax refund each year? Think about changing your deductions to keep more of your income instead of letting the IRS use it for a full year before giving it back to you.

2. Redirect your cash flow. Often you can redirect money currently going into poorly performing or risky market investments into a 7702 Plan™.

3. Make your money go to work for you. Often funding a plan with extra money you've got in the bank makes sense because you are getting guaranteed growth and still have access to it.

4. Get off the roller coaster. This may be a no-brainer if you have money in stocks or mutual funds. Consider moving some money out of the market if you are tired of the roller coaster.

5. Withdraw from 401(k) and IRA. IRAs and 401(k)s could become a tax-time bomb when you start taking money out. They often have exposure to the stock market downturns as well. Your 7702 Plan™ may allow you to eliminate unknown taxation when you start taking distributions and can secure your money from risk in the market. (Please consult with your tax professional and a qualified advisor before withdrawing from qualified plans.)

6. Stop the expenses. When they add it all up, people are often shocked at how much extra they are paying in insurance, utilities, and other everyday expenses. Making some minor lifestyle changes, or just doing a little research on reducing current expenses, can help you build up your 7702 Plan™ and get on the path of Safe Money.

7. In force insurance policies. Many people have existing life insurance policies that are not structured as effectively as possible. You may be able to do a

1035 exchange that keeps the cash value and the tax benefits you currently have while improving your results.

8. Chopping away at debt. Instead of slowly chopping away at debt, consider funding a 7702 Plan™ and then taking a chunk of money and paying off the balance of a credit card. This could save you a substantially amount on interest costs.

9. Splurge on your future. Instead of taking the money from your tax return and buying that big screen TV or trip, consider funding a 7702 Plan™ and building on your financial future.

10. Extra mortgage payments. If you are currently making extra payments to your mortgage principal, consider putting that into a plan where growth is guaranteed while also giving you access to that cash without having to qualify for a loan in order to use it.

"Good question. This is the true beauty of the Safe Money 7702 Plan™—it allows us to put money away and know with relative certainty how much is going to be there for you when you need it."

Susan chimes in. "Yeah, I'm really tired of opening our 401(k) statement and seeing it go down, down, down!"

"Usually, a 7702 Plan™ performs best the longer you let it grow and compound. When do you think you will want to start taking money out?" Michael asks.

"Well, let's say age 65," Jason replies.

After crunching a few numbers, Michael says, "Assuming that you get average growth of 7-8% using the indexing strategy (we'll cover this in a second) at the age of 65, you could have right around $800,000, with a death benefit of approximately $1.1 million that could go to your spouse or children. But here's the real exciting part . . . are you ready?" [25]

"Yeah. What have you got?"

"Using these projections, at age 65, you could have an annual cash flow, that you can access without a taxable event, of $97,000 until age 100."

"$97,000 per year . . . that I get without a taxable event? Wow, that's amazing, especially considering it's not going to get wiped out in a market downturn, and we know we can count on it being safe," Susan says.

"$97,000 per year for 35 years is like 3 million dollars! How is that possible?" Jason says.

"Remember that when you borrow against your policy, the cash value continues to grow as if it's never been touched. It's also important to remember these projections are done using the insurance companies' actuarial projections. They use data from the past 25 years . . . but they aren't guaranteed. There's a chance it could be less than that."

Susan jumps in. "I appreciate you saying that. I hate to be sold a bill of goods only to be disappointed. Even if it's half that amount, having about $45,000 per year to live on until age 100 is pretty fantastic. Plus, that money isn't at risk in the market. But $1000 might be pushing it for us right now. What would happen if we only did, say, $500 per month?"

"No problem," Michael says. "With $500 per month, you're still potentially looking at $48,000 every year until age 100. You don't pay tax on this money because you are borrowing against the policy, not withdrawing the money out of the policy. Of course, this is the way it works under the current IRS tax laws.

"Keep in mind," continues Michael, "these policies work with compound interest. That means that the more money you put into your policy, the faster your policy grows. Why wouldn't you want to put as much money as much as possible into a policy that only gets better the more you put in? With traditional investments like 401(k)s or mutual funds, there is no direct correlation between the amount you contribute and improving results. A 7702 Plan™ gets better as you contribute more and more. In fact, it grows exponentially, meaning the growth maximizes when you need it most during your later years."

"Interesting. So we should consider finding ways to increase the amount we pay in because we'll get better results that way?" Susan asks.

"Exactly," Michael adds. "Plus, don't forget that you can access that money without having to pay taxes on it under the current IRS tax codes—as long as you structure the policy correctly. That's why working with a trained Safe Money Associate is so important. If you don't do it right, you could lose major tax benefits or miss out on maximizing your cash value growth. This is too important to trust to someone who hasn't had the proper training."

As we step away from the table, it is clear that Jason and Susan are off to a good start on their journey to retiring with Safe Money. But as we leave them to the beginning of their new financial life, we have some shocking revelations to show you.

In the next chapter, we'll show you what might just be the most exciting part of this whole process.

Jason and Susan can potentially have such a great cash flow in retirement because they are using the Indexing strategy with a 7702 Plan™. This allows them to participate when the market goes up . . . but never risk their money to loss when it comes down. That's exactly what you'll see in the next chapter.

CHAPTER 8

SUPER CHARGING
THE 7702 PLAN™

"The first rule of investing is NEVER LOSE MONEY.
The second rule is NEVER forget rule #1."
— Warren Buffett

I've always wanted to fly. Not in a plane, hot air balloon, or with the help of something man-made. I simply want to look up and take off flying through the air. Unfortunately, I haven't figured out how to make that happen—like the old saying goes: "What goes up must come down." I learned that the hard way jumping off the bunk bed as a kid.

As we've discussed, this up-and-down phenomenon is not limited to physics—it happens quite frequently on the stock market as well. We can have some exhilarating rides up only to suffer financial broken bones when the market comes crashing back down. But it doesn't have to be that way. In this chapter, I'm going to show you how you may just be able to defy market gravity.

One of the most exciting things about a 7702 Plan™ is that you can supercharge the cash value portion of your insurance policy by using a special indexing strategy. The indexing strategy can allow you to enjoy the upside growth of the market without ever risking your money to market losses! (You can go up without coming down!)

In other words, the 7702 Plan™ indexing strategy could give you double-digit returns on up years when the market gains, without the downside risk!

This means when the market goes up, your money can grow (I'll explain more in just a second) *but when the market goes down, you are protected and your money cannot be lost.* This can be extremely beneficial during times of market turbulence. In years when the market goes up, so do your cash values, and when the market falls, you are protected against that loss. Your money is locked in so you don't lose!

Now, why is this so important?

Because inflation is one of the biggest threats to growing your money and wealth. If inflation is running at 3-5% (or even higher, depending on the government's monetary policy) it's important to have your money outpace inflation.

If your money is growing slower than the rate of inflation, you aren't growing your money—you are actually decreasing the value of it over time! The indexing strategy can allow you to outpace inflation by capitalizing on potential double-digit growth in the years when the market goes up.

Wait a minute.

Didn't I just spend several of the first chapters in this book explaining why the stock market may not be the greatest place to invest your money? Am I changing my tune?

Not at all.

The cash value growth in your 7702 Plan™ indexing policy is *linked* to the S&P 500 or some other index of your choice, but your cash is *not* actually invested *in* the market. That way, your money is always safe and guaranteed by the insurance company.

Remember in Chapter 2 when we showed you the different plunges the market had taken over the years and how long it took to recover and return to even? Now you don't have to deal with that at all!

Your money is protected from any market loss because it is not directly in the market, but at the same time, you participate in the growth of the S&P 500 up to a limit or cap. Let's say the upside cap is 12% (this can vary from plan to plan). This means even if the market goes up 14% or more, your cash value growth would be limited to just 12%.

Having a cap is actually a good thing because this is what allows the insurance company to protect you against losses in those years when the market goes down.

Let's look at a picture that will illustrate this point. This is a hypothetical example of a typical stock market strategy vs. a 7702 Plan™ indexing strategy.

So, let's say you start out with $10,000. And in the first year, the S&P 500 grows by 10%. The first year, there is no difference, and you have $11,000 in either account. In year two, your money grows another 10%. Now you have $12,100 in either account.

Index Strategy vs. Market Strategy

But let's say that in year three, the S&P 500 drops 20%. Can that happen? Sure it can. The last few years of the 2000s were worse times than that! Now you would have about $9,600 if had you invested directly in the S&P 500. However, in the indexed strategy, your principal and interest are protected against market loss. So, now instead of $9,600, you hold at $12,100.

In year four, the market drops another 17%. Now, instead of having $9,600, you have around $7,900. In the indexed strategy, you're still on hold at $12,100.

Now here's the million-dollar question: Do you want $7,900 or $12,100?

That's quite a difference, and it's clear from this example that losing principal can be financially

Index Strategy vs. Market Strategy

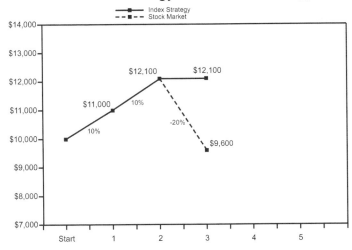

devastating. That's why Warren Buffet said, "It's not so much about the return *on* your money as the return *of* your money." When you lose principal, you've got to get big-time results to bring it back to even.

Index Strategy vs. Market Strategy

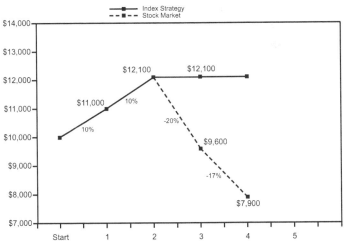

Now let's look at what happens when the market rebounds. Let's say in year five, the market grows by 15%. In the stock market strategy, the $7,900 would get the full 15% growth, which is about $1,100, so your cash value would climb back up to a little over $9,000. In the indexed strategy, your money would only grow by 12% (remember we have a cap) to $13,550. But even with the capped growth, you have $13,550 versus $9,000!

Again, quite a difference.

Index Strategy vs. Market Strategy

In this example, the downsides of the stock market strategy were:

- After five years, you end up with less money than you started with.

- From the end of year 4 to year 5, it would take a 30% return to get you back to your original $10,000 (and how likely is that to happen in *one* year?)

- Even if you did get the 30% you needed, it will only bring you back to $10,000. You just lost *five* years and you are just barely back to even.

Can you see why the 7702 Plan™ indexing strategy is so exciting? Now you can have your money growing when the market goes up, you could outpace inflation with potential double-digit gains, and you never have to worry about losing money when the market goes down.

What kind of peace of mind would that give you, knowing that your money is always safe?

Now what would happen if the market goes down for 10 years in a row?

Many of the 7702 Plan™ policies can be set up so that there is a guaranteed amount of growth credited to your policy cash values, which guarantees that even if you don't achieve growth in the market, your cash value can continue to grow. (Every plan is a little bit different. That's why it's so important to work with a trained Safe Money Associate who can show you your options.)

The rest of the 7702 Plan™ benefits still work the same. Meaning, you can Finance Your Own Prosperity™ by accessing your cash value for cars, college, or other major purchases. *Some financial products can even guarantee an income you will never outlive.* Be sure to ask your Safe Money Associate about this!

Now, with all this being said, indexed life insurance doesn't have to be where you put all your money, but for many people, it is an excellent way to position a portion of your portfolio to enjoy the ups of the market without the downside risk.

This is obviously a brief introduction to the indexing strategy. To learn more about how this works, just request a 7702 Plan™ Blueprint at the end of this book and a Safe Money Associate can help you see it in action and answer your questions.

To Sum It Up

The indexed strategy makes sense for people who want to avoid market risk, but still want the possibility of double-digit gains and all the other benefits that a 7702 Plan™ can give them.

Using this strategy, you could save more money even without changing your current lifestyle by repositioning some of your assets from being deposited into accounts that are taxed during retirement to an indexed life insurance policy.

The supercharged 7702 Plan™ indexing strategy could allow you to:

- Participate in double-digit gains in up years

- Help outpace inflation

- Grow your money tax deferred

- Access cash values without incurring tax

- Provide cash flow for life

In the next chapter, we'll show you exactly how cash value life insurance impacted the lives of men and women just like you. You'll also recognize some of the biggest names in business that used their cash value life insurance to build their wealth.

Turn the page to see if you recognize a few of these people who, like many of our Safe Money retirees, used the living benefits of life insurance to grow their wealth.

SECTION 4

DOES IT WORK?

"People seldom improve when they have no other model but themselves to copy after."

— Oliver Goldsmith

CHAPTER 9

DISNEY, J.C. PENNEY, MCDONALD'S, AND YOU: MAKING IT WORK

"Though no one can go back and make a brand-new start, anyone can start from now and make a brand-new ending."
— Carl Bard

Holly is a 42-year-old New Yorker and a single mother of two. She has a steady job working in an HR department, earning about $33,000 per year, and is having a hard time making ends meet.

Her two kids are in the "expensive" stage of life—middle school and high school—where it seems like every time you turn around, there's another expense.

She's running ragged taking care of two kids, working full-time, paying the bills, and keeping the house in order.

It's almost too much for any one person to handle.

Add to it the fact that she's in a seemingly insurmountable amount of debt, and Holly doesn't feel like she's ever going to get out of the hole she's in.

She sees no light at the end of the tunnel—no way out!

But it gets worse.

She was actually in more debt than she realized. After totaling up all the credit cards, lines of credit with stores, and the student loans, her debt total, not including her car or home, was over $59,000. She knew it was bad, but this was a real eye-opener. That was two years' worth of her salary, and $59,000 did not even count her car or home debt.

She was contributing $100 per month to a company retirement plan, but she knew that was not going to give her the financial independence she wanted.

The rest of her paycheck each month was going to pay bills or pay down credit card and student loan debt.

When we asked her what three financial goals she had, her reply was a lot like you might guess. First, she'd like to have a little money set aside to take a break and breathe for a weekend or so.

Next, she wanted to get out of debt and have some emergency savings put away just in case something came up with her or her kids.

And lastly, she wanted to be able to save money for her kids' college funds and her own retirement.

With only $33,000 in income, $59,000 in consumer debt, and college loans, two kids, and a mortgage, doesn't this seem like a hopeless case?

Left to her own devices, she really was hopeless. She didn't know what to do, and she didn't feel there was any way out of her current situation.

That's where we came in. After reviewing her debts, expenses, and current retirement contributions, we helped Holly put together a 7702 Plan™, which included a spending and debt analysis. Through that process, we helped Holly find and put away over $500 per month she didn't know she had.

Over $500 per month on just a $33,000 per year salary!

Plus, she was able to redirect her current retirement contributions that were currently at risk in the market into an indexed 7702 Plan™ insurance policy to create a nest egg she can count on. She has literally started down the Safe Money path to retirement.

This might seem hard to believe, but the exciting part is that based on the insurance company projections, by the time she turns 65, she could potentially take out $68,000 per year, every year until age 100! Plus, as long as she does it properly, that money can be accessed without incurring tax!

Imagine her relief when we gave her the 7702 Plan™ Blueprint that showed her how, using just her current income, she could create a simple plan to follow.

This process helped her get out of debt, get her spending under control, and ultimately, gave her hope because she now has a plan for financial independence.

By steadily putting away money each month, she could have the security of knowing that after age 65, she could have as much as $68,000 per year on just a $33,000 income! Plus, when she does pass on, she'll have a death benefit payable to her two children because of her life insurance policy!

JC Penney

In 1898, James Cash Penney was working in a Golden Rule Store, which was one shop in a small chain of dry goods stores. He turned out to be such an enterprising worker that the pair of owners took him under their wing, offering him a one-third partnership in a new store they were opening. James managed to scrape together $2,000—a pretty significant sum in those days—and opened the new store in Kemmerer, Wyoming.

During the next five years, James helped open two more stores and was doing very well. James focused his efforts on the stores, even investing the extra money he made by working as a lumberjack. By 1912, he was running 34 stores throughout the Rocky Mountain region.

The next year, James moved his company headquarters to Salt Lake City, Utah, and incorporated under a name you'll easily recognize: The J.C. Penney Company. The chain exploded and by 1929, there were 1,400 stores throughout the nation.

Then things got interesting. The stock market crashed, and the nation was plunged into the depths of the Great Depression. The Depression devastated his stores and his wealth. He was in financial ruin.

Luckily, James had not risked all of his money in the market. He had built a Safe Money foundation. To rebound from the difficult times, he took out a loan from his cash value life insurance policies. He used the cash to meet day-to-day and payroll expenses for his chain of stores. Not only did he keep his head above water, but he also rebounded. Today, the stores take in revenues nationwide of $18.5 billion a year.

As it turns out, that simple cash loan had a greater impact than even James could have realized. Ever heard of Walmart? On a 1940 visit to a J.C. Penney store in Des Moines, Iowa, James patiently trained a young employee, Sam Walton, showing him how to gift-wrap packages using the least amount of ribbon needed to do the job—and another retail giant was born.

Dr. Jeff

Jeff thought he was doing pretty well.

He was fifty years old, making a great income as a doctor, and putting $1,000 into his 401(k) every month. On top of that, Jeff had over $110,000 already socked away. Of course, he wasn't really thrilled that he'd recently lost a big chunk of it in the market crash of 2008, yet despite this setback, he thought he was still on track for a great lifestyle.

He wanted financial independence at age 60, and he figured if he could have $70,000-$80,000 per year to live for the rest of his life, he could hang it up whenever he wanted to after 60. He was also afraid inflation was going to continue to eat away at his savings. Jeff wanted to make sure that he could provide his own retirement cash flow. He didn't want to count on social security because, according to the Congressional Budget Office, in 2011 the Social Security Administration was already running a 45-billion-dollar deficit. And at the end of the day, he wanted to be in control of his finances and retirement, not leave it to someone else.

You could say Jeff thought he had it all under control. In his mind, he was doing everything right. Until he saw the truth.

You see, most people have no idea how long their money will actually last after they stop working.

Jeff crunched some quick numbers. He already had $110,000 saved. Plus, he was adding $1,000 per month to his 401(k). The result was shocking. He discovered that if he continued on his current path, he would only have about $30,000 per year during retirement. And this was BEFORE taxes! Assuming he's in a 28% tax bracket, that's more like $23,400 per year or $2,000 per month!

Right now Jeff is living off $10,000 per month, so living off just $2,000 per month was like a cold bucket of water right in the face.

But that's not all.

There are other problems with Jeff's current plan.

The money in his current retirement plan is fully taxable. Like we already showed above, the $30,000 gets taxed when he pulls it out to use it. Plus, if he dies before he retires, his income stops and he won't have the money built up to provide for his wife or family— there are no guarantees or death benefit. The money is at risk in the market, and the money is tied up in a qualified government plan.

But it gets worse.

This is what really shocked him: For his 80th birthday present, he would be looking at an empty retirement account! That's right—his $2,000 per month would be gone by the time he was 80.

Remember, Jeff wants to retire at age 60.

Using the Lifestyle Income Estimator on our www.21stcenturyfinancialservices.com, we showed him that his $2,000 per month could actually run out in less than 20 years!

According to *US News and World Report*, once a man reaches 65 years old, his life expectancy is 83 years, and one in every four will live past age 90. [26]

He wondered what type of lifestyle he was going to have with just $2,000 per month, living with the fear that the money would run out all too soon.

So, we looked at some other options for him.

By using a 7702 Plan™ and working with an Safe Money Associate—a specialist in helping people secure cash flow that they won't outlive—we came up with a solution that excited and delighted him.

Jeff wanted to see what his retirement would look like if he redirected the $1,000 from his 401(k) into an indexed cash value insurance policy.

We also showed him how to use a rule in the tax code to roll some of his money out of his 401(k) without penalties. He could then use this money to fund his indexed cash value insurance policy, which would safeguard his money against market downturns. (This needs to be suitable for the client.)

He was comfortable using one of our 7702 Plan™ Insurance Companies because this particular one has been around for over 300 years and has nearly 600 billion dollars in assets around the globe.

After implementing the 7702 Plan™ indexing strategies, Jeff was amazed and excited at his new financial independence plan.

Remember, in his current situation, he was looking at running out of money after 15 to 20 years. Plus, this income was fully taxable, didn't have any guarantees, and it was at risk in the market.

With the Indexed 7702 Plan™, his new plan could give him approximately $69,000 per year—for the rest of his life! And as long as he follows the IRS code properly, he could access that cash flow without a taxable event (according to current IRS tax code).

But that's not all.

In his new 7702 Plan™, he has no market risk, and if he dies too soon, his family will be protected with the life insurance death benefit. Plus, he has access to the cash value in his insurance policy to finance himself to wealth throughout his life!

Like we mentioned before, Jeff was excited about $70,000 per year compared to $24,000, and delighted when he saw this new plan. Wouldn't you be?

What if you are already in your late fifties or even sixties and don't have a plan like Jeff has? Is it too late?

Thankfully, it's not. There are still many options for people of any age, but it's important to start now, and not let another day go by without implementing the Safe Money plan. Get started today at:

www.21stcenturyfinancialservices.com.

Walt Disney

The second household name you'll no doubt recognize involves a man who fought all odds to follow his dream: Walt Disney. [27] Walt and his brother, Roy, were in the animation business. Their story is almost hard to believe. One of their most popular characters was stolen by another studio. Their best animator jumped ship. Their studio was chronically understaffed and almost always in debt. In fact, Walt Disney struggled financially for years on the brink of bankruptcy—actually going bankrupt at the age of 21.

Fast-forward to the early 1950s. The only amusement parks in the entire country were horrifically dilapidated places peppered with rusting, creaky rides and known only for their filthy restrooms and the drunks who always hung around. Walt dreamed instead of an immaculately clean amusement park filled with imaginative rides—a place where families weren't afraid to eat the food. World War II had just ended, and the nation was licking its wounds. Walt dreamed of creating an amusement park with an idealistic Main Street, U.S.A., where families could identify with something wholesome and good. But that's not all: he dreamed of charging admission to his park and actually making a profit.

Everyone to whom he presented his idea thought he was crazy—and told him so. After all, *no one* charged admission to an amusement park. That just wasn't done. And amusement parks simply couldn't be family-friendly— everyone knew you'd have to sell alcohol if you wanted a prayer of staying afloat. Even his brother Roy—also his business partner and financial manager—told him it couldn't be done. He urged Walt to forget it. After all, they were in the animation business, not the amusement park business.

Determined to achieve his dream, Walt had no choice but to move ahead on his own. Turned down by traditional financing, he emptied his savings account, sold his vacation home in Palm Springs, and recruited the help of a few employees who shared his vision. Then, he used a loan from his cash value insurance policies to help finance the park. (Roy later admitted he had no idea where Walt's money was coming from, but decided not to ask.)

What happened to Walt's dream? Disneyland opened on September 8, 1955, with 18 attractions. It welcomed half a million visitors in the first month it was open. By the end of its first year, it had hosted more than 3.5 million guests. Less than three years later, it welcomed its ten millionth visitor—a number that exceeded well-known national landmarks like Yellowstone and the Grand Canyon. Today, its California park alone—with more than 60 attractions—has been visited by more than 600 million guests from throughout the world. A dozen of the original attractions from 1955 are still operating in the park today as a testament to Walt Disney's dream of a high-quality, enduring adventure for families.

Robert G.

Robert distinctly remembers the day he first knew that nothing could stop him. He had landed a great-paying sales job, and he was also less than a year away from graduating with a degree in business. He was finally on his way up.

It had been a busy year for Robert. In fewer than 12 months, he had sold his old home—for a tidy profit—and finished building his family's new home. Just as they were unpacking the boxes, his wife announced that they were expecting a baby. They were delighted! Robert knew life would change, and that his cost of living would go up with another mouth to feed, but the idea of his growing family only motivated him to work all the harder.

Life seemed to be moving in the right direction for Robert.

He'd been with the company for almost a year when the recession of 2008 caused the economy to plummet. The medical specialty that Robert served was hit particularly hard. Things started to get tough. His income was going down, but his costs weren't.

With his wife at home, caring for their new baby, and with only one income to support the family, money became tight for the first time in their marriage.

Robert went from comfort and a sense of security to just the opposite. In just 12 months, he went from having $15,000 in the bank to having $15,000 in credit card debt. He went from the joy of building a new home to the fear of losing that home. He went from a feeling of being unstoppable to a gripping sensation of worry. He despaired of ever being able to climb out of debt and replace his savings.

Robert now had an empty bank account, a whopping credit card debt, two ailing cars, and a home on the verge of being foreclosed. He faced the embarrassment of losing his house, disappointing his family, and starting over. The last straw was his final few weeks at his job—his last three paychecks bounced because the company didn't have the funds to pay him.

Sound hopeless?

It could have been. But something changed for Robert—and it's the same kind of thing that can change for you. He went back to the drawing board.

Robert's biggest paradigm shift was realizing the difference between saving and investing: *saving* is putting your money where you don't risk losing it. *Investing* is putting your money where you might lose it all.

Robert also wanted to grow his money while protecting it from taxes. He finally found the solution he was looking for: a 7702 Plan™. He took what little money he received from his tax refund and started a 7702 Plan™. Despite the terrible economic situation, it changed his entire outlook.

In his own words: "I could create a crystal-clear picture of what my financial future would look like. I could have money in case of emergency or capital in case a good investment opportunity came up. I could use my 7702 Plan™ to pay for vacations, get out of debt, and send my kids to college or pay for my retirement.

"A 7702 Plan™ gave me a sense of security and gratification, knowing that my money would grow and be available for my use and that my family would be protected and taken care of in case something should happen to me. I have an idea of what my future will look like, I know how much money I will have at certain milestones in my life, and I have a strong financial foundation on which to continue building."

Doris Christopher

Doris Christopher may not be a name you recognize, but the company she founded will be very familiar. Doris was a successful home economist and educator, but she had a dream. All those hours working with homemakers had convinced her that women needed quality timesaving tools designed to make cooking quick and easy. Women didn't want to spend hours and hours in the kitchen grinding out meals—they wanted to create great meals, quickly, due to their increasingly busy schedules.

Doris not only had a dream—she had a plan.

Doris's plan involved an army of consultants who would do in-home cooking demonstrations using her professional-quality tools and equipment. Tupperware had done it, and with outstanding success—a homemaker schedules a party, invites her friends, and the rest falls into place.

With the support of her husband, Jay, and that of her two young daughters, Doris came up with a detailed business plan and got ready to put it into action. The only thing standing between her and her dream was money.

Her solution was simple. In 1980, Doris borrowed $3,000 from her life insurance policy, and The Pampered Chef® was born in the basement of her suburban Chicago home.

In the ensuing decades, the business moved to a series of progressively larger facilities. By 2002, the company had blossomed into a $700 million enterprise that was acquired by Warren Buffett's Berkshire Hathaway Corporation. Today, The Pampered Chef® has grown into a multimillion-dollar international corporation serving 12 million customers annually—and it all started with the loan from her life insurance policy. [28]

Angie

To protect her privacy, we won't tell you Angie's last name— but her life insurance advisor, Rocky, is happy to tell a convincing story about another aspect of the 7702 Plan™: the legacy we leave to our family when we pass on.

Angie was married to Michael—a 41-year-old anesthesiologist. They were referred to Rocky by another physician, and Rocky met Angie and Michael at their home to discuss their needs. They had a young family— three children under the age of seven. Together they determined they needed $2 million in life insurance coverage.

After a second meeting, during which Michael filled out all the applications, Rocky also signed him up for $10,000 a month in disability insurance.

Everything went well for the next 18 months. Suddenly, Michael started getting sick. His weight plummeted. He became so weak that it was a struggle to work. A battery of tests revealed no cause for his medical problems, and he became desperate. Almost out of options, he finally talked to a colleague who suggested a latex allergy as the possible culprit. Michael was tested, and sure enough, he was allergic to latex. His allergic reaction was behind the host of symptoms that had plagued him.

With a confirmed latex allergy, Michael had to stop working in the hospital. His disability insurance kicked in, providing an income of $10,000 a month. Yearning to still practice medicine, Michael used some of his disability income and part of his cash value life policy to start a pain clinic—a clinic with a strict ban on latex of any kind.

Things went very well for two years. One night, Angie went out to dinner with friends. Michael, who wasn't feeling well, stayed home. That night, Angie found him dead on the bathroom floor. The autopsy results revealed that Michael had contracted bacterial meningitis—and because of the impact that his latex allergy had on his immune system, he didn't have the ability to fight the infection. It killed powerfully and suddenly.

Shortly thereafter, Rocky delivered a $2 million check to Angie—the amount of the death benefit on the cash value life policy she and Michael had purchased just a few years earlier. Nothing can bring Michael back, but Rocky felt a great sense of satisfaction in helping provide a secure financial future for Angie and her children as a result of their life insurance policy.

Ray Kroc

Ray Kroc came from humble beginnings. Born in Chicago in 1902, at the age of 15, he lied about his age and landed himself a job as an ambulance driver for the Red Cross. Later, he actually trained to become an ambulance driver during World War I (where he struck up a friendship with Walt Disney, who was in the same training). Peace treaties were signed before he saw any combat action, so he returned home and tried his hand at a number of jobs—paper-cup salesman, pianist, jazz musician, band member, and radio disk jockey. In a move that would later prove fortuitous, Ray worked at a restaurant in exchange for room and board so he could learn the restaurant business.

In 1954, at the age of 52, as a milkshake machine salesman, Ray took notice of a hamburger stand in San

Bernardino, California. While most restaurants bought one or two Prince Castle Multi-mixers which could each mix five shakes at once, the San Bernardino restaurant had bought eight. Curiosity got the better of Ray Kroc, and he wanted to see what kind of restaurant needed to churn forty milkshakes at a time. And so he set out for California.

What Kroc saw when he got to that restaurant—a hamburger stand owned by Maurice and Richard McDonald—would not only change his life forever, but would change the scene of the fast-food industry throughout the world.

Kroc saw the two legendary golden arches and saw lines of people queued up for the restaurant's simple fare of burgers, fries, and milkshakes.

Ray Kroc wanted to slow down as a traveling salesman. His health was declining. He was suffering from diabetes and arthritis, and he had bigger fish to fry. Ray managed to convince the brothers to sell the McDonald's name and trade secrets to him, and worked a deal to pay for it with a percentage of the receipts.

McDonald's was on its way to becoming a household name. In 1955, Ray opened his first McDonald's drive-in restaurant in Des Plaines, Illinois.

While things inside the restaurants ran smoothly, Ray faced massive challenges with cash flow, franchises, competition, and the economy in general. He was determined to be successful and spent year after year, working day and night, to build his company.

In order to build the largest fast-food chain in the world and overcome constant cash-flow problems, Ray took out loans on two cash value life insurance policies to get his infant company off the ground. He used some of the money to create an enduring advertising campaign that centered on the company's mascot, Ronald McDonald.

Ray Kroc passed away from old age in January, 1984, at the age of 81, just 10 months before McDonald's sold its fifty-billionth hamburger. At the time of his death, there were some 7,500 McDonald's restaurants worldwide. Today, with more than 25,000 restaurants worldwide, McDonald's is the world's largest food-service retailer, with operations in more than 65 countries.

To Sum It Up

What did you learn from James Cash Penney, Dr. Jeff, Walt Disney, Stephen G., Doris Christopher, Angie, and Ray Kroc? There are important lessons in every one of these examples. You can work as hard as humanly possible. You can make all the right plans. But when the financial storms come, if you have a weak financial foundation, it can be devastating. But if you have the right Safe Money foundation in place, you can withstand them. You can keep your money safely growing outside of the market. You can have the peace of mind you are looking for.

And here's the really great news. It's not hard or complicated. You don't have to know it all.

To see a personalized blueprint of how a 7702 Plan™ could work for you and your unique situation, just use the form in the back of this book or go to www.21stcenturyfinancialservices.com and fill out a 7702 Plan Blueprint Analysis request, and a Safe Money Associate will work with you to design a custom 7702 Plan for you and your family—*at no cost.* This blueprint can show you how to get on the Safe Money path by helping you get out of debt, save on taxes and eliminate the risk of losing your money in the stock market. By creating a safe money foundation, you can Finance Your Own Prosperity™ and control your financial future.

Remember what you learned from Aristotle in the opening pages of this book: "Money is a guarantee that we may have what we want in the future."

You may not be able to go back in time and change your beginning, but you can start today and make a brand-new ending.

CHAPTER 10

GOD'S MIRACLE:
I'VE BEEN RESTORED!

by Terry Keyzer

"My wealth has come from a combination of living in America, some lucky genes, and compound interest."
— Warren Buffett

I was born on September 8th, 1945, to a dairy farmer and his wife in Delavan, Wisconsin. My father started out his career as a sharecropper, but by the time I was in my teens, he had saved enough to purchase his own farm. He wanted me to go into the business with him, but his idea of training involved fists and straps, and that wasn't for me. I decided to go my own way instead.

As I grew up, I never wanted for anything, but I didn't have all the latest and greatest things, either. My parents had been raised during the Great Depression, and they were frugal. They made do with what they had and repaired things when they broke. They made everything last.

I attended school in a one-room building my first four grades, but then I went to Delavan Christian School and Elkhorn High. I never did graduate from Elkhorn. When I was seventeen, my mother signed a permission slip, and I enlisted in the Air Force. I earned my GED while I was in the service.

I served my country for four years and was honorably discharged in 1966. In 1967, I was introduced to the life insurance business, and I did that part time for the next thirteen years.

In 1980, I went full time as a field agent for NASE, and within a year, I was promoted to state manager. I had written a policy for a family in Green Bay, Wisconsin, and they sent a letter to the company, thanking them for sending that persistent agent to their home. Their mother had a stroke, and if I had not signed them up, they would have had to sell their business and their home to pay the bills.

That day, I realized that I was helping people! Up to that point, it had been a struggle—I was only thinking about my income. Now it was easy, as I was helping people and it wasn't about me anymore.

In 1985, my wife, new son, and I moved to Florida, where I started working with Surety Life. I soon rose to the top, and in 1988, Tom Chester, the president of Surety Life, asked me if I would like to move back to Wisconsin as a regional director. My wife and I accepted the offer and moved, now with two sons.

In 1990, we started developing the state, opening agencies and hiring and training agents. We did this until Surety quit their marketing department. In 2000, we sold out in Wisconsin and moved back to Florida.

At this point in my life, I had everything—a plane, a boat, a nice home. We weren't keeping up with the Joneses'—we were showing *them* how to live. I had too much, and I didn't know how to handle it all. I started drinking, and alcohol took everything from me. My scorecards all read zero. I'd drink and drive, get in trouble with the law, and have to sell a house in order to fix the mess. Soon, I ran out of houses to sell, and after my fourth DUI, my wife left. My kids weren't talking to me, I had nowhere to live, and I was sleeping either on my boat or at friends' houses.

I'd been told by several judges that I should start going to AA, but I hadn't done anything about it. That is, until May 28th, 2005. I'd finally had enough. I walked into an AA meeting and heard the voice of the Lord speaking directly to me: "If you're obedient, I will restore you." And He did.

God had a mission for me. I've started over completely, and now I'm a ministry leader for Celebrate Recovery. I teach others how to overcome and be sober just as I was taught. A little at a time, I was able to put my life back together, including healing my marriage and family.

After a few years in recovery, I was dabbling with farming and insurance, and my wife was working long hours as a nurse. We decided that I should go back to insurance full time.

For years, I looked at various opportunities and companies. Nothing looked good. Then finally, Federal Financial Group reached out to me and I went to their convention, and that was the beginning of this chapter in my life. Their products are sound, and their reasons for being in business—helping people—matched what I was looking for.

As I've had the opportunity to work with FFG and train new agents, I've discovered that the principles I use to help others overcome alcoholism are principles that can be used in all areas of life. As I was growing up, I wasn't given a blueprint for how to live my life, but Alcoholics Anonymous gave me a format for what a decent person should be doing—helping others—and that's what I teach my agents. People helping people is what it's all about.

Chapter 11

Bonus:
For Business Owners Only

*"The entrepreneur is our visionary, the creator in each of us.
We're born with that quality and it defines our lives as we
respond to what we see, hear, feel, and experience."*
— Michael Gerber

If there's a portion of the country that is underserved and underappreciated, it might just be the small-business owner.

I know firsthand because I have been one for the better part of a decade and my family has a long genealogy of small-business owners.

It goes all the way back to my great-great-grandfather, who was a tavern owner in Germany.

From there, we have my great-grandfather, who owned several farm and ranch-related businesses, and my grandfather, who owned several construction businesses. Being a business owner is tough.

I know what it's like to have the stress of overhead, payroll, advertising to get new clients, economic forces outside of our control, the late hours, missed soccer games or music recitals, and the huge amount of risk we take on. We do it all because we want to provide financial security for our families and live the American Dream of financial success.

Most of us don't get benefit packages that someone else is paying for. Usually no one is contributing to *our* retirement plan. We don't punch a time clock or have the luxury of having someone else cut us a check every two weeks. It's common knowledge that the small-business owner is the engine of the American economy. Yet too often, we work ourselves to death and continually pour any extra money back into the business, often neglecting our own savings as we try to build our companies.

If you are anything like me, we approach our business with a case of never-ending faith that next week, month, or year, we'll make the money we want. And soon, months and years have passed, and we've invested everything back in the business and haven't stashed anything away for ourselves.

Joining the ranks of the Safe Money plan owners could change that right now.

Not only can a 7702 Plan™ create an "automatic safe money machine" where you put money away each month without thinking about it, but you can still access that money for use *in* your business.

Let's talk about three simple ways you can be using a 7702 Plan™ to save money, prepare for the future, and help your business grow.

Finance Your Own Prosperity™

If you buy equipment, vehicles, own real estate for your business or investments, or provide a service, this is for you.

Funding a 7702 Plan™ can be done a couple different ways.

You can start by simply putting in a set amount of money each month, then borrowing against that cash value to buy whatever you need for your business.

You can also start a plan by dumping in a one-time payment like $20,000, $50,000 or even $100,000 and using that as your own source of funding. It's kind of like your own private source of financing, except no qualifying is necessary to use the cash!

Use your 7702 Plan™ to buy business equipment, vehicles, or real estate by using the money in your plan while it still grows as if you've never touched it. Instead of going out and buying a truck for your company the old way, use your 7702 Plan™ to finance your purchase, then recoup the cost of the truck by paying your insurance loan back.

You can even get more advanced by using these plans as a separate entity that acts as a leasing company that purchases vehicles, real estate, and other equipment.

If the Worst Should Happen

Ever heard of a business getting destroyed because a partner dies and the spouse comes in to take over the interest with no experience whatsoever?

I really do like my business partner's wife, but she and I running a business together would not be a pretty picture.

It happens more often than you might think.

In fact, take a look at these sobering statistics.

These figures show the likelihood, out of 100, that one of two business partners in good health will die prior to 65:

Age of Business Owners	Chances
40/40	35%
45/45	33%
50/50	29.9%
55/55	24.7%

If there are three partners, the percentages are much higher. [29]

So what does that mean for you and your business? If you have a partner, or two, you can use a 7702 Plan™ insurance policy to fund a buy-sell agreement. This would provide you with cash to buy out that partner's ownership of the business if they should die. The company can continue to thrive without the disruption of a new partner and the spouse of the partner will be compensated fairly.

But it gets even better than that.

Let's go for the best-case scenario. Assume you and your partner both live long, healthy lives.

You get to enjoy all the living benefits of the 7702 Plan™ throughout your lives the same way we already have described previously. Use it for vehicle financing, major purchases, funding growth, or buying real estate.

Ride Off Into the Sunset

This is ultimately where you probably want to be.

We've hopefully already established in black and white why a solid foundation of safe money is the key to a great lifestyle— but why not use this powerful tool to grow your business, save you money on interest throughout your life, and then enjoy a passive stream of cash flow that comes from your 7702 Plan™ as you travel to exotic destinations with your spouse, golfing the days away and enjoying the fruits that you worked so hard for?

If all the living benefits weren't enough to convince you that a 7702 Plan™ should be a part of your financial plan, this might.

Willie Sutton and the Tax Man always follow the money.

> "The single biggest benefit in the tax code is the tax exemption for life insurance."
> Ed Slot
> The Retirement Savings Time bomb

Depending on current laws, estate taxes can take a chunk out of your estate, which could include residential and commercial real estate, investments, and all the assets you may have. Often people underestimate their estates, and yet they can add up to $800,000 to $1,000,000 fairly quickly.

Imagine the problem your family could have when they get a tax bill saying they owe $500,000 and much of that is tied up in real estate.

This is especially problematic if the real estate market is down, and people have to "fire sell" at below market value just to satisfy the demands of the Tax Man.

Here's where the 7702 Plan™ really shines.

Under current IRS tax code, life insurance proceeds are paid out income-tax free. This means they come to the estate, or your family (depending on how the policies are set up) in a lump sum. You can use that money to pay the estate taxes while protecting your other hard-earned assets. Life insurance payouts *are* usually subject to estate taxes, so keep that in mind when you calculate how much insurance you'll need to cover the entire tax bill . . . and as always, consult with a proper estate tax planning professional.

This is where a Safe Money Associate could really help you. Not only can they help you with a 7702 Plan™, but also with asset protection, estate tax planning, and other issues to help build a strategy for protecting and growing your wealth. Just go to:

www.21stcenturyfinancialservices.com

to request a free 7702 Plan™ Blueprint for Business Owners Only. A Safe Money Associate who has gone through an extensive amount of training on structuring these plans can help you achieve all your goals now to protect your legacy.

Free Bonus Content

Free 7702 Plan™ Blueprint Analysis Talk with a trained professional who can show you in black and white how to create the financial independence you are looking for.

Lifestyle Income Calculator Discover how long your income will last living the lifestyle you want.

Safe Money For Business Owners See how the 7702 Plan™ can protect your business, build your wealth, and save taxes.

All on: www.21stcenturyfinancialservices.com

Acknowledgements

Brent

I would like to acknowledge my two associates and friends, Brett Kitchen and Ethan Kap, for their help on this book.

Terry

When I was very young, our landlord, Mr. Jackson, spent hours with me teaching me how to work with numbers. Numbers became my friend. This was a valuable lesson to me.

My father, George Keyzer, taught me there's no such thing as "can't." The lesson I got out of that statement was, any task put in front of me, I could do. No matter what the obstacle, the task could be accomplished. I just had to apply myself and never give up until it was done.

A quote from Napoleon Hill: "What the mind can conceive and believe, you can achieve."

My favorite verse from the Bible is Deuteronomy 31:8. "The Lord Himself goes before you and will be with you; He will never leave you nor forsake you. Do not be afraid; do not be discouraged."

My AA sponsor Bobby Leone has always been there, no matter what, with encouragement and wisdom while I was sobering up and getting my life back together.

My wife, Virginia, six children, twelve grandchildren, and two great-grandchildren stood by my side as much as they could, as my alcoholism put them through hell. I've been sober over ten years now, and things are improving little by slowly.

Confidential 7702 Plan™ Blueprint Analysis
(Use black ink, please)

Name: _____

Address: _____

City, State, Zip: _____

Primary Email Address: _____

Day Phone: _____ Evening Phone: _____

Best time to reach you: _____

Were you referred by anyone: _____

Please rate your priorities from 1 to 5 (1 being the most important):

_____ Having an income for life

_____ Keeping your money safely growing outside the market

_____ Having fast access to your money . . . on your terms

_____ Getting out of debt

_____ Financing your own prosperity

To best prepare to help you, please tell us about yourself:

Age: _____

Occupation: _____

Income: _____

Do you own your home? YES or NO

Years left on mortgage:_____ Balance on mortgage: _____

Do you own a business? _____

IMPORTANT: Your information is accessed by Safe Money Associates so they can provide your analysis.

We ask for your phone number and email to be able to provide your 7702 Plan ™ analysis to you. Your Safe Money Associate will design a custom 7702 Plan ™ that may help you reach your financial goals. By filling out and returning this form, you are giving our advisor permission to contact you.

Send your request to:

Safe Money 7702 Plan Blueprint
c/o Terry Keyzer
W 2899 Otter Lane
Rib Lake, WI 54470

ENDNOTES

1   *Federal Reserve Board, 2004*

2   *Cardweb.com*

3   *60 minutes, 401(k) Recession, Ira Rosen*

4   *US News and World Report; 7 Retirement Risks You Need To Prepare for, April 2, 2010. Emily Brandon*

5   *Become Your Own Banker, 2008, Nelson Nash*

6   *FDIC.gov; Foreclosure statistics*

7   *AFL-CIO analysis of 292 companies in the S&P 500 Index. CEO pay data provided by salary.com.*

8   *Barry James Dyke, Pirates of Manhattan*

9   *Nelson Nash, Becoming Your Own Banker*

10   *Barry James Dyke, Pirates of Manhattan*

11   *http://news.bbc.co.uk/2/hi/business/3746044.stm, Monday, 1 November, 2004, news.bbc.co.uk*

12   *http://www.kiplinger.com/magazine/archives/2008/05/hidden-401(k)-fees.html#ixzz13CwvXJKI*

13   *Damien Hoffman, "Cramer Buy Recommendation CIT Goes Bankrupt," Wall St. Cheat Sheet, Nov. 1, 2009.* 136 Safe Money Millionaire

14   *Bill Alpert, "Cramer's Star Outshines His Stock Picks," Baron's, Feb. 9, 2009.*

15   *Ira Rosen, "The 401(k) Fallout," 60 Minutes*

16   FBI History, Famous Cases, Willie Sutton, *www.fbi.gov*

17   Scott Shultz, *www.avoidthedeferraltrap.com*

18   William Wolman and Anne Colamosca, *The Great 401(k) Hoax: Why Your Family's Financial Security Is at Risk and What You Can Do About It (Cambridge, MA: Perseus Publishing, 2002), 12.*

19   "The Outer Limits, Some of These Funds Go Way Beyond the Ordinary," Forbes, September 18, 2006.

20   Anthony Mirhaydari, MSN Money The following adapted from Barry James Dyke, *The Pirates of Manhattan: Systematically Plundering the American Consumer and How to Protect Against It (Hampton, NH: 555 Publishing, Inc., 2008), 69–76.*

21   *http://www.livinghistoryfarm.org*

22   *http://blogs.wsj.com/deals/2010/11/08/tracking-bank-failures- 2010-tops-2009-for-bank-failures/*

23   Pirates of Manhattan, Barry James Dyke

24   Ed Slott, *The Retirement Savings Time Bomb . . . and how to diffuse it.*

25   Based on illustration of 42-year-old male, preferred health, using an A Rated Indexed Life Insurance Company illustration using a 5.7% variable loan rate and 8.7% monthly growth cap.

26   *http://finance.yahoo.com/focus-retirement/article/110176/ predicting-your-life-expectancy?mod=fidelityreadytoretire&cat=fidelity_2010_getting_ready_to_retire*

27   Adapted from Catherine and Richard Greene, *The Man Behind the Magic: The Story of Walt Disney (NY: Viking Penguin, 1991).*

28   (Currency/Doubleday, 2005) and Come to the Table: A Celebration of Family Life (Warner Books, 1999).

29   *http://www.raricklaw.com/assets/pdf/client-newsroom/2009/*

ABOUT THE AUTHORS

Terry Keyzer got his license to sell insurance in 1967, working the business part time until 1980, when he became a full-time agent. He retired in 2000, but a series of life events brought him back into the industry in 2013.

At that time, Terry hooked up with Federal Financial Group and turned his life around financially, while AA turned his personal life around. He now counsels others on their paths to recovery.

Terry lives with his wife in northern Wisconsin, and together they have six children, twelve grandchildren, and two great-grandchildren.

Brent Tycksen is the president of a national financial marketing organization with over 70 offices in 30+ states and over 3,000 agents.

Brent has been in the financial services industry since 1978. His passion is helping people grow and protect their wealth from all the financial cancers that afflict us—taxes, market risk, interest exposure, etc.

He and his wife live on a small farm in Salem, Utah, USA where they raise alfalfa, chickens, and beef cattle.